A

PRACTICAL

COMPANION

TO

ETHICS

A
PRACTICAL
COMPANION
TO
ETHICS

Anthony Weston

New York   Oxford
OXFORD UNIVERSITY PRESS
1997

OXFORD UNIVERSITY PRESS

Oxford New York
Athens Auckland Bangkok Bogotá Bombay
Buenos Aires Calcutta Cape Town Dar es Salaam Delhi
Florence Hong Kong Istanbul Karachi
Kuala Lumpur Madras Madrid Melbourne
Mexico City Nairobi Paris Singapore
Taipei Tokyo Toronto

and in associated companies in
Berlin Ibadan

Published by Oxford University Press, Inc.
198 Madison Avenue, New York, New York 10016

Oxford is a registered trademark of Oxford University Press

Library of Congress Cataloging-in-Publication Data
Weston, Anthony, 1954-
A practical companion to ethics / Anthony Weston
p. cm.
Includes bibliographical references.
ISBN 0-19-510534-6 (alk. paper)
1. Ethics. I. Title.
BJ1025.W43 1997
170—dc20 96-10558

1 3 5 7 9 8 6 4 2

Printed in the United States of America
on acid-free paper

Contents

—𝔪—

Preface

—ᙢ—

One of Einstein's "three great laws of work" is that every difficulty is also an opportunity. This "law" is certainly true in
ethics. Finding a way that is whole-hearted and right can be
very hard indeed, but it is also an opportunity for our most
creative and responsive thinking. The aim of this book is
simply to help its readers make more of that opportunity.
You may find—I hope you do find—that a little help can go a
long way.

In order to keep the text as uncluttered as possible, I
have left all citations and suggestions for further reading to
the Notes and Comments sections at the end of each chapter. Some of the more philosophically controversial points
made in this book are a little more fully explained and
defended, for those who may have questions or objections,

in the Notes and Comments as well. Interested or provoked readers might consult my book *Toward Better Problems* (Philadelphia: Temple University Press, 1992) for more fully developed philosophical accounts.

I have tried to write in such a way that this book can be used either in a classroom or as a self-sufficient reader for anyone who might be interested. I have therefore gathered the specifically classroom– and course-oriented points into two appendixes. The first is for students and offers specific advice for writing an ethics paper. The other offers some advice to teachers: suggestions for teaching with this book.

Peter Williams, Tom Birch, and Nim Batchelor stand out for special thanks among the many friends and colleagues who contributed advice and encouragement to this project. Donald Becker (University of Texas at Austin), Earl Conee (University of Rochester), Peter Markie (University of Missouri), and several other philosophers served as publishers' reviewers. I very much welcome any comments or suggestions that readers may have.

Raleigh, North Carolina   A. W.
June 1996

Introduction

This book is an invitation to ethics. It is meant to fill the gap between the theoretical issues common in the ethics of philosophers and the practical questions of the doubter and the newcomer. One question is: who even *needs* ethics? Another is: why think for yourself? These are real questions, and they need to be answered before the rest of ethics—its theories and its methods and its history—can speak to us.

This book also aims to bring out the connections between ethics and certain useful methods in practical thinking generally. For example, there is a large literature on creative problem solving: on multiplying options and reframing problems so that the original problem is transformed. There is an equally large literature on conflict resolution and compromise, crucial skills if we are to avoid polarizing values and the people who hold them. This book brings all of these skills into the spotlight.

Finally, this book is concerned with the heart. Too often I have seen students come away from an ethics course knowing a lot about the theories of ethics and how to apply them in specific cases, but with little sense of the deeper call to responsiveness and care that underlies these formalities. In fact, responsiveness and care are crucial. Some of the most intriguing developments in contemporary ethics begin right here: we could think of the new ethical awareness of other animals, for example, as nothing less than an experiment in open-heartedness.

This, then, is a *practical companion* to ethics. It is meant as an essential supplement to the usual first presentation of ethics, and as an essential skill-book as one goes on in ethical practice. It invites, explains, improves, expands. It places ethics against a larger practical background in order to clarify its role and its potential. It aims to uncover creative possibilities where we now seem to have only dilemmas and intractable conflicts. It seeks to open both our minds and our hearts.

It may seem odd that such a book is necessary at all. Why can't the great theories of ethics, or the many textbooks and collected readings in ethics, explain ethics well enough by themselves?

The answer is complex—also controversial—and not something we can expand upon here. I will say only this. A better invitation to ethics is necessary because most of the main works in ethics tend to take the need for ethics for granted. This is not exactly an objection—the main works in auto mechanics and dance theory take the need for auto mechanics and dance theory for granted too—but it does leave gaps. A supplement can help. Otherwise, ethics may seem too academic, or too much trouble. Why think for yourself, and invite social disapproval and uncertainty, when you can just take the word of the dominant authority figures? Why think at all, when we can just consult our feelings? Really, why?

Standard ethics books also seldom discuss the how-tos of ethics: how to frame a problem so that it can be most effectively solved; or how to deal effectively, interpersonally or politically, with fundamental ethical disagreements; or why and how feelings matter. Many philosophers prefer to concentrate on ethics' unique intellectual challenges. But most people come to ethics to learn how to *live*. This is a far broader question. And in truth it poses a rich mix of challenges too, to the imagination and to the heart as well as to the head. It may be that by concentrating on certain intellectual challenges unique to ethics, we tend to slight the practical (and creative and imaginative) skills that are vital to ethics but *not* unique to it. So part of the aim of this book is to rejoin ethics to life skills—to put ethics into its rightful place.

This book therefore does not duplicate the many histories and applications of ethics already available. It only rehearses in the briefest way the usual theories and their advantages and defects and applications. This book is intended instead to offer some practical orientation and problem-solving skills, to open up some creative space within the usual formalities, and to give them a heart. It is, again, a *companion* to ethics.

Some of the advice offered in this book may seem obvious. If it does, just remember that we are much better at giving advice to others than at recognizing when we need it ourselves. Actually, we need the advice too, sometimes even the simplest advice. We need the reminders. Moreover, even when a mistake is obvious, how to carry on in a better way—how to avoid the mistake next time—may not be obvious at all. It may take time and care to develop the necessary skills. Give them the time and the care they need. They will repay your efforts—many times over!

A
PRACTICAL
COMPANION
TO
ETHICS

1

Getting Started

—ᴍᴍ—

WHO NEEDS ETHICS?

Why isn't it enough to follow our feelings or "fly by instinct" when we are thinking about what we should do or how we should live?

Feelings are essential, of course. A life without love, excitement, and even pain is no life at all. No livable ethic denies this. But feelings are not the whole story. They may be the beginning, but they are not the end. A certain kind of *thinking* must also be part of the story.

Take prejudice. To be prejudiced is to have a strong negative feeling about someone who is of a different ethnicity or gender or age or social class (or . . .) from yourself. If ethics were just a matter of feelings, then there would be nothing to say against such prejudices. It would be perfectly ethical to discriminate against people you don't like.

Instinct says yes. But ethics says no. Ethics instead may challenge these very feelings. "Prejudice" literally means "pre-judgment": it is one way of not really paying attention. But we need to pay attention. We need to ask why we feel as we do, whether our beliefs and feelings are true or fair, how we would feel in the other person's shoes, and so on. Only by thinking these feelings through carefully can we begin to recognize their limits and then, if necessary, change them.

So ethics asks us to think carefully, even about feelings that may be very strong. Ethics asks us to live *mindfully*: to take some care about how we act and even about how we feel.

There is another contrast with "flying by instinct." Instincts and feelings may oversimplify complex situations. We want things to feel clear-cut even when they are not, so we may persuade ourselves that they are. Mindful thinking, by contrast, is more patient. Where things are really unclear, feeling may even have to wait. Premature clarity is worse than confusion. We may have to live with some questions a long time before we can decide how we ought to feel about them.

Our feelings are also easily manipulated. For instance, it is easy to be swayed either way by "loaded" language that plays upon our emotions. Define abortion as "baby killing" and you create a negative feeling that closes the case against abortion before it can even be opened. But fetuses are not babies (look the words up). On the other hand, if you describe abortion as no more than "minor surgery," you suggest that it is both unintrusive and even healthy. It isn't. Either way, we are led into a prepackaged emotional commitment without ever thinking it through. Habit and conformity take over.

Mindful thinking, by contrast, is more complex and open-ended. It is in this spirit that ethics approaches controversial issues of the day, like abortion or professional ethics or the status of other animals. We do care for other animals, for instance. But we also use many of them for food, shoes, chemical tests, even as objects of sport. Should all of this stop? No? Well, should any of it stop? Probably. So what uses of other animals should stop and what kinds should not? Why? How do you decide?

These questions cannot be intelligently answered by just consulting your feelings. There are too many different possibilities, too many different "uses," too many different opinions and prejudices (on all sides) that need to be carefully sorted out. Again, it takes some time and care. Maybe even some degree of compromise.

Every ethical issue discussed in this book is another example. I will try to suggest that much more intelligent and creative thinking is possible about these issues than we usually suspect. But the key word is "thinking." Ethics invites us to try.

SOME COUNTERFEITS

There are many ways in which we are tempted to avoid ethical mindfulness. We need to be warned against some of them here.

Dogmatism

A dogmatist is someone unshakably committed to one answer to an ethical question, or perhaps one answer to all ethical questions. *Which* answer is not so clear: dogmatists (rather ironically) tend to disagree. Dogmatists do agree, though, that careful and open-ended thinking about ethical issues is not necessary. If you already know the answer, there is no need to think about it. Struggle and uncertainty, according to the dogmatist, are not a necessary part of ethical thinking (or daily life either, I guess).

How does dogmatism arise? One way is this. We are often told that having doubts, especially about your moral positions, is a form of weakness. Instead, moral seriousness is supposed to require unshakable principles, absolute conviction. But consider what this position means if it is carried to its logical conclusion. If you need to argue for your position, you admit that it needs defending, which is to say that people can legitimately have doubts. But that can't be true: you already know that your position is the only right one. Therefore, any reasoned argument for your position is unnecessary. And any reasoned argument against your position is obviously, without a second thought (or even a first thought), absurd. So, why listen?

This much is right about dogmatism: being committed to a certain set of values—living up to them, or trying to, and sticking up for them when we can—is a fine thing. It is not a fine thing, though, to be so committed to them that you cannot see any other side, and cannot even defend them beyond simply asserting and reasserting them (more and more loudly, probably). This is a pitfall, a trap. You can no longer even think. This is the trap that ultimately leaves us pleading "My mind is made up; don't confuse me with facts."

Ethics, once again, paints a different picture. Despite the stereotypes, the point of ethics is not to moralize or to dictate what is to be done. Ethics is not another form of dogmatism. The real point of ethics is to offer some tools for thinking about difficult matters, recognizing from the start—as the very rationale for ethics, in fact—that the world is seldom so simple or clear-cut. Struggle and uncertainty are part of ethics, as they are part of life. This is what makes life hard. It is also what makes life so intriguing, sometimes so beautiful, and so full of possibility and promise.

Just being consistent is sometimes hard enough. For example, people who are actively pro-animal often also favor legal abortion. But is it consistent to defend the helpless in one case and not in both? On the other hand, people who oppose abortion on the grounds that all life is sacred often also favor the death penalty. Here the question is much the same. If all life is sacred, isn't a murderer's sacred too? Besides, if you really believe that all life is sacred, shouldn't you also be a pacifist and a vegetarian?

These questions may well have answers. Some people have recognized and addressed the seeming inconsistencies. The point is only that the answers are not obvious. There is no escape from some open-ended thinking.

Rationalizing

Another enemy of the ethical is what I call "offhand self-justification." This is the strategy of the rationalizer.

Suppose that a person states some moral position. Suppose, moreover, that this position is stated dogmatically, that is, stated as obvious, not open to any kind of question or reconsideration, and certainly never questioned by the dogmatist him– or herself.

But then suppose that some challenge arises. A friend who cannot be brushed aside unexpectedly disagrees. A child who has not yet learned politeness keeps asking "why?"

For a moment, the façade is threatened. The dogmatist has never actually had to offer a reason before. Does our dogmatist now admit doubt and uncertainty? It's not likely. Instead dogmatists scramble to save face: to find plausible-sounding reasons to back up their original overstatements. That is, they rationalize.

The problem is that such off-the-cuff reasons are unlikely to be very good reasons—which is even more likely to be pointed out, leading to another cycle of challenge, embarrassment, defensiveness, and eventually anger. In a class debate, for example, one of my students fervently insisted that it is not immoral to kill animals for food. Asked why, he first seemed puzzled, then quickly announced, "Because they have four legs rather than two like us." Clearly he was casting around for a reason, and this was the first reason he could think of. Unfortunately, it was a bad one. He had no idea why number of legs should make any difference to the treatment of a creature. He had also forgotten that some other two-legged animals—chickens, for example—are also killed for food in massive numbers.

There may well be good reasons for this student's position. The point is that the quick rationalizer is not going to find them. Notice that the result is actually worse than merely holding one unintelligent opinion. When we rationalize, we saddle ourselves with more and more unintelligent opinions—new ones invented, off the top of the head, to patch up the holes in the old ones. But the new ones, like the two-legs excuse, are likely to be full of holes as well. It's not a winning game.

Better to just stop, admit some uncertainty, and think about the question some more. It is not necessary to have an opinion about absolutely everything, and it is certainly not necessary to have an absolute opinion about absolutely everything!

Relativism

Relativism may simply consist of the observation that different individuals and societies sometimes have different standards. Some people recycle everything, while others can barely get their litter in to a trash can. Some societies care a great deal about sexual self-control among the young; others care very little. Captain Cook, arriving in native Hawaii in the 1770s, was amazed to discover that the Hawaiians cared much more about unmarried young people eating together than sleeping together.

Relativists usually go on to conclude that no one single standard is right. Sometimes relativism in this sense is entirely appropriate. If you don't like raspberries, you don't have to eat them. You are not "wrong" (maybe unlucky—but, of course, that's only my view). Even in ethics a little relativism is sometimes useful. Sometimes we need to fend off moralizers, for example. Sometimes we need to assert our right to do as we please, even if others think we are making a big mistake. And beyond the practical level, there are deep issues about truth and consensus that some philosophical forms of relativism help illuminate.

Relativism becomes damaging, however, when it becomes another way to resist careful and open-ended thinking in ethics. For example, someone may insist that ethics is a purely personal matter, no one else's business. Another form of relativism insists that any ethical opinion is as good as any other. These views slide quickly into offhand self-justification. If critical questions can simply be dismissed with a wave of the hand or the warning to "mind your own business," then it is too easy never to think critically at all.

For example, suppose I claim that you should never trust a doctor to make a life-or-death decision, because (I say) doctors are more interested in their fees and their reputations than in patients' needs. You challenge my opinion by pointing out that many doctors do not fit this stereotype. I cannot just reply that "Any opinion is as good as any other" or "Who is to say that I am wrong?" or even "Let's agree to disagree." I really am wrong—not always, not about all doctors, but surely about some. You're entitled to say so. And I need to rethink and revise my opinion and learn to give some doctors the benefit of the doubt.

The same goes for ethical opinions based on any form of careless thinking. If I generalize about all members of some ethnic group based on just one, or refuse to consider the possibility that my actions make other people or other creatures suffer, or excuse my polluting ways on the grounds that the whole environmental crisis is a hoax, I am not entitled to use some kind of relativism as an excuse to simply close down any discussion and close off any challenge. I need to defend my opinion and the beliefs and reasoning behind it. I need to open-mindedly consider the evidence and counter-evidence, and change my mind if necessary.

And this is a simple point, really. In truth we all know it already. Relativism (the damaging kind) just goes too far. Standards do apply. The same old requirements of mindfulness and care remain, even if they do not settle all disagreements. Values may differ—values are indeed relative in that sense—but the fact that values may differ does not excuse us from trying to do better with the values we have.

"Mind your own business" is an antisocial response as well. Issues like pollution, for example, affect all of us. Poisoned air goes into all of our lungs, poisoned water through all of our bodies. On the other hand, the money spent on pollution cleanup and prevention could also go for other things, perhaps better things. For some people it could be a life-or-death matter, however we decide. The same goes for issues like professional ethics, abortion and assisted suicide, treatment of other animals, and many other ethical issues. None of these are just matters of personal preference. None of them are just our own business. These matters—basic ethical issues—are everyone's business.

Some philosophers argue that this is the very point of

ethics: to help us arrive at certain standards that we all are to live by when all of us are affected by each other's behavior. On this view, ethics is precisely for those cases where "mind your own business" doesn't work as an approach to a problem. Instead, we need to work things out together. We need to think things through carefully, use evidence responsibly, and talk it out. And that, I have argued, is where ethics starts.

Notes and Comments

The view that values essentially reduce to feelings is sometimes called "subjectivism." This term, however, tends to have many different and even incompatible meanings, often depending on whether or not the person using the term agrees with the view being described. Take care with it. For a discussion and critique of various meanings of "subjectivism" in ethics, see "Ethical Subjectivism," in *The Encyclopedia of Philosophy*, Vol. 3 (New York: Macmillan and the Free Press, 1967), pp. 78–81.

On dogmatism, see Stephen Pepper, *World Hypotheses* (Berkeley: University of California Press, 1942), chapter II. It is worth noting that dogmatism is possible both on the large scale and on the small. Some people hold all of their opinions dogmatically and others only a few, but both are at least to some extent dogmatists. The same holds for rationalizing. Probably all of us rationalize at least sometimes.

Rationalizing may be one of the deepest of all pitfalls in ethics (and in life generally) and deserves a chapter of its own in any fuller treatment. For some psychological background, including some fascinating and unsettling experiments, see David Myers, *Social Psychology*, 4th ed. (New York: McGraw-Hill, 1993), chapters 2–4. For a useful overview of self-deception, see Mike Martin, *Everyday Morality* (Belmont, CA: Wadsworth, 1995), chapter 6.

For some suggestions about how to avoid rationalization and self-deception and how to deal more effectively with dogmatists, see the section "Some Suggestions for Classroom Practice" at the end of this book.

I use the debate about other animals as an example of rationalizing for several reasons. One reason is that it is an issue of genuine concern and interest to many students, despite the impatience and dismissal their concern often meets from some scientists and dining-hall administrators. Most introductory textbooks in philosophy now have some discussion of ethics and animals. For a brief survey of the philosophical debate and a critique from the point of view presented in this book, see my book *Toward Better Problems: New Perspectives on Abortion, Animal Rights, the Environment, and Justice* (Philadelphia: Temple University Press, 1992), chapter 4. Another reason for turning to this topic is that it seems to offer uniquely fertile ground for rationalization. Maybe we're especially sensitive to issues about what we eat.

There are almost as many characterizations of relativism as there are people who write about it. For a survey, see "Ethical Relativism," *The Encyclopedia of Philosophy*, Vol. 3, pp. 75–78. A kind of relativism not mentioned in the text is "cultural relativism," according to which values are relative to one's society. This view too comes in a variety of forms and has a variety of problems. It is certainly true that our values are influenced by social norms. This does not mean that they just *are* social norms (otherwise, for one thing, social norms could not be criticized ethically) or that they are somehow just social inventions that have now been unmasked and can be safely ignored (since there may be good *reasons* for social norms).

My responses to the challenge of relativism as I have defined it are deliberately minimalist. I have tried to offer responses that can be advanced in good faith by philosophers with otherwise widely varied views. For example, whatever else is true, it is at least true that most ethical matters are matters of public concern, one way or another, where some intelligent way of going on *together* is necessary. Ethical philosophers may develop this response in a variety of directions. The social contract tradition in ethics tries to derive a substantive ethics from this very characterization of the point or origin of ethics. For influential contemporary accounts, see John Rawls, *A Theory of Justice* (Cambridge, MA: Harvard University Press, 1971), Sections 3 and 20-26, and David Gauthier, *Morals by Agreement* (Oxford: Clarendon Press, 1986).

Relativism may sometimes be more plausible with respect to issues that (seem to) affect only the individual. Here lie some of the more hotly debated issues at present, like sexual preference, pornography, and suicide. It might be argued in response that some of these activities—for example, viewing pornography—do affect or endanger others. Other ethical theories raise other sorts of problems, even if the behavior is agreed to affect only oneself. The would-be relativist must at least examine these reasons. "Mind your own business" might be an appropriate position on some issues, especially in a society committed to tolerance and diversity. Still, on any particular issue, the appropriateness of relativism is something that has to be *shown*. Reasons, once again, must be considered. Actually, that's the moral of the whole story: reasons must *always* be considered!

2

Thinking for Yourself

—ᚥ—

From the start, we look to others for guidance: parents, teachers, role models. As adults too, we turn to family and friends for advice and help. We look to our religious, philosophical, and political traditions as well. This is how we learn many of our values in the first place, and how they change or deepen over time. And this is how it should be.

It is also possible, however, to go too far. It is one thing to rely on others for advice and help. It is quite another thing to let others decide for us. Ethics asks us to think for ourselves.

APPEALS TO AUTHORITY

There are three common kinds of appeals to authority in ethics:

- There are appeals to social norms. The appeals may be to the authority of other people or of society or of tradition. Do it, we're told, because "it's what's done."
- There are the orders and commands of leaders or bosses.
- There are appeals to God—which are, in practice, either appeals to religious authorities and spokespeople or to authoritative texts such as a religion's bible.

In each of these cases, we get the message that we have something much stronger than mere advice or help. When authority is invoked, it is ours just to obey. Do what's expected; follow orders; obey God. Thinking and deciding for ourselves are not required. Indeed, when this attitude is carried to the extreme, we may be specifically required *not* to think or decide for ourselves.

In fact, however, we have a responsibility to think for ourselves. None of the common appeals to authority can take the place of our own careful and open-minded consideration.

Take social norms first. Certainly social norms are often wise. Certainly we may find much to respect in them. Still, they are also not infrequently products of long habits of prejudice, closed-mindedness, even repression—not wise at all. Don't forget that sexism and racism were, and in many ways still are, social norms. Yes, so are politeness and basic courtesy. But so are timid conformism and a suspicion of any new ideas. In fact, social norms are a mixed bag: not to be ignored but certainly not the last word either.

Likewise, the orders of our leaders or bosses can be wrong. We know from recent cases of whistle blowing on corporate and public-service abuses—illegal pollution, shoddy or lethal products, police corruption, and so on—that abuses do happen, and that there are strong pressures not to make them public: indirect threats and the tugs of group loyalty, as well as direct threats and orders to keep quiet. In response to this problem, many organizations are taking steps to protect whistle blowers and to allow them to bring forward their complaints within the organization itself. Corporations themselves acknowledge that their own norms, and even the direct orders of superiors, are not and should not be absolutely binding.

The orders of political and military leaders can be wrong too. During the trial of Lieutenant William Calley for war crimes at the Vietnamese village of My Lai in 1968, *The New York Times* reported the testimony of James Dursi, a rifleman in Calley's company:

> Lieutenant Calley and a weeping rifleman named Paul Meadlo . . . pushed the [villagers] into the ditch. . . . "There was an order to shoot by Lieutenant Calley, I can't remember the exact words—it was something like 'Start firing'. Meadlo turned to me and said: 'Shoot, why don't you shoot?' He was crying. I said 'I can't. I won't.' Then Lieutenant Calley and Meadlo pointed their rifles into the ditch and fired. People were diving on top of each other; mothers were trying to protect their children. . . ."

Dursi disobeyed a direct order to shoot. Yet he was right. In general, even when we are given a direct order to do something, it is still our responsibility to decide whether to follow it. This principle has repeatedly been affirmed in war crimes tribunals. It is not enough to say "I was just following orders."

Religious Authority

Appeals to religious authority seem rather different. God— by definition, some would say—cannot be wrong. God is conceived as omniscient and perfectly good. Therefore, the commandments of such a God are surely compelling: surely better than our own partial knowledge and dubious goodness, necessarily the proper reference point for our ethical action. Appeals to God look like a clear-cut case of a compelling argument from authority.

In fact, things are not so clear. There is, of course, the problem that religions differ. One religion's God may say one thing; another religion's, another. This at least implies that appeals to one religion's God cannot settle matters when people of other religions (or no religion) are involved. This is why church and state are separate in America: we are a people of many religions who meet and live together on common, and therefore neutral, ground.

But there is a still deeper and more fundamental difficulty. Appeals to God, in practice, are never actually to God. Instead, they are appeals to some religious leader who claims to speak for God or to some religious text that claims to be the true word of God. And this inevitably means the reentry of human claims to authority into the picture.

This is quite a different matter. God may be perfectly good, but there are no guarantees about anyone else. Established religions may mirror the distorted and backward social norms just mentioned. Despite the heroism of some individual ministers, for instance, white churches were not notably out in front in the civil rights struggle (not notably behind, either, but that's just the point: they reflected their society). Historically, many churches supported slavery. Every religion's bible, meanwhile, is the product of a long history of human translation, editing, argument, even persecution and centuries of war. Scholars believe, for instance, that the first five books of the Christian Old Testament—which also form the Jewish Torah—represent not one voice but the work of at least three different writers, woven together later by still other writers. Later still they were translated—from Hebrew to Greek, from Greek to Latin, from Latin to English—and are still read very differently by Jews and Christians.

In fact, then, appeals to the "word of God" are inevitably appeals to human interpretations, human arguments, and human points of view. This is true even if you believe that they are inspired ultimately by God. These appeals, as we have already seen, cannot be the last word. They may have much to offer—sometimes they may even offer us the very best that human tradition can offer—but still, even then, they cannot simply be put in place of our own judgment.

The Problem of Ambiguity

Another problem with appeals to God's authority, especially when we appeal to a sacred religious text such as a bible, is that bibles are often ambiguous. The stories are more complex than we are encouraged to think, and the morals of the stories are much less clear.

Here is one example. Some Christians insist that the Bible condemns homosexuality. One common scriptural reference is to the story of the destruction of Sodom. Read the story:

> The two angels came to Sodom in the evening; and Lot was sitting in the gate of Sodom. When Lot saw them, he rose to meet them . . . and said, "My lords, turn aside, I pray you, to your servant's house, and spend the night, and wash your feet; then you may rise up early and go on your way." . . . He urged them strongly; so they turned aside to him and entered his house; and he made them a feast, and baked unleavened bread, and they ate.
>
> But before they lay down, the men of the city, the men of Sodom, both young and old, all the people to the last man, surrounded the house, and they called to Lot, "Where are the

men who came to you tonight? Bring them out to us, that we may know [i.e., rape] them." Lot went out of the door to the men, shut the door after him, and said, "I beg you, my brothers, do not act so wickedly. . . . Do nothing to these men, for they have come under the shelter of my roof. Behold, I have two daughters who have not known man; let me bring them out to you, and do to them as you please; only do nothing to these men, for they have come under the shelter of my roof." But [the crowd] said, "Stand back!" . . . Then they pressed hard against Lot, and drew near to break the door. But [the angels] put forth their hands and drew Lot into the house to them, and shut the door. And they struck with blindness the men who were at the door of the house, so that they wearied themselves groping for the door. (*Genesis* 19:1-11)

God destroys the city the next day after helping Lot and his family to flee.

This story is complicated and confusing. God does destroy Sodom, so clearly there is something that He means to condemn. But what? The text does not say. The traditional reading is that the true crimes of Sodom are its shocking level of violence and its extreme disrespect for strangers. The prophets Isaiah and Ezekiel specifically refer to the sin of Sodom as the sin of injustice, oppression, and pride. On this view, homosexuality has nothing to do with it.

We might suppose that if anything is specifically condemned in this story, it is rape. After all, rape is what the crowd had on their minds, and the crowd, along with the city it stands for, is quickly punished. But here too things are confusing. In fact, this is almost the only clear condemnation that the story does *not* make. Lot, who is presented as the only relatively decent man in Sodom, actually offers the crowd his own daughters in the place of his guests. The angels prevent these rapes too from happening. But God still saves Lot from the destruction of the rest of the city. Does not Lot's treatment of his own daughters offend God? Is the shelter of his roof for strangers more important than the shelter of his roof for his own children?

We are reminded that this story was written at a time when values were very different than they are now: when, for one thing, women were regarded only as a man's (father's or husband's) property, for him to dispose of as he saw fit. Again we see the intrusion of human prejudice and blindness into what is supposed to be the word of God. Regardless of what the story does or does not condemn, then, we might have doubts about its true moral authority.

In any case, again, we are left unclear about just what it is that God condemns about Sodom. That it is homosexuality is a major leap—added, we might suspect, by people who already oppose homosexuality and are looking to Scripture for support. But in that case we need to hear and evaluate their reasons, not a forced reading of Scripture to make it yield the desired conclusion. Perhaps there are good arguments, but a facile reference to the story of Sodom is not one of them.

THINKING FOR YOURSELF: A BIBLICAL MODEL

This is our responsibility: to think for ourselves. Once again, I don't mean that we must never listen to others. Listening to good advice and thinking about new perspectives are crucial. Religious texts too have long been sources of great inspiration and stimulation: use them. But then it is still up to us to interpret, ponder, and decide.

It may help to keep in mind another part of the Sodom story—a part very seldom cited in appeals to God's authority, but a part nonetheless, and in fact right next to the episode just quoted. Just before the angels visit Sodom, they visit the patriarch Abraham in his desert tent. As they leave, they declare God's intention to destroy Sodom if the rumors about it are true.

Abraham is troubled by this. He cannot see the justice of killing the innocent along with the wicked. So Abraham, says the Bible, "went before the Lord." He actually took it upon himself to question God!

> Abraham drew near and said: "Wilt thou indeed destroy the righteous with the wicked? Suppose there are fifty righteous within the city; wilt thou then destroy the place and not spare it for the fifty righteous who are in it? Far be it from thee to do such a thing, to slay the righteous with the wicked, so that the righteous fare as the wicked! Far be that from thee! Shall not the Judge of all the Earth do right?"
>
> And the Lord said, "If I find at Sodom fifty righteous in the city, I will spare the whole place for their sake." Abraham answered, "Behold, I have taken upon myself to speak to the Lord, I who am but dust and ashes. Suppose five of the fifty righteous are lacking. Wilt thou destroy the whole city for lack of five?" And He said, "I will not destroy it if I find forty-five there." Again he spoke to him, and said, "Suppose forty are found there." He answered, "For the sake of forty I will not do it." Then he said, "Oh let not the Lord be angry, and I will speak. Suppose thirty are found there." He answered, "I will not do it, if I find thirty there." He said, "Behold, I have taken upon myself to speak to the Lord. Suppose twenty are found there." He answered, "For the sake of twenty I will not destroy it."
>
> Then [Abraham] said, "Oh let not the Lord be angry, and I will speak again but this once. Suppose ten are found there." The Lord answered, "For the sake of ten I will not destroy it." And the Lord went his way, when he had finished speaking to Abraham; and Abraham returned to his place. (*Genesis* 18:23-33)

What is the Bible telling us here? Surely not that we should simply do what we're told, and accept whatever authority decides to do. Quite the contrary! Abraham, the revered forefather, did not simply obey. He would not accept injustice even when God Himself proposed to do it. He went to God ("I who am but dust and ashes") and complained. He questioned, he challenged. "Shall not the Judge of all the Earth do right?"

Abraham thought for himself. Moreover, he was honored for doing so. God listened and answered. Indeed Lot himself was saved, the Bible says later, because God was "mindful of Abraham" (*Genesis* 19:29). So the next time someone acts as though it is ours only to obey the dictates of God (according to them) or the dictates of some other authority— remember Abraham!

THE QUESTION OF RULES

Similar to the appeal to authority is the appeal to rules—or, more exactly, the appeal to what are supposed to be hard and fast moral rules. Here too we are told that our task is not primarily to think for ourselves but to obey. Here too, however, what we are told may not be the whole story.

Like the advice and guidance of others, rules—of a sort, anyway—are crucial. Life is too complicated to think everything through from the beginning. We have to rely on rules of thumb: rough and ready provisional guides that allow us to get on well enough most of the time: "Better safe than sorry"; "Better late than never"; "If it's not broken, don't fix it."

Still, these rules are *rough* guides. They have exceptions. Sometimes late is worse than never. Safety may become such an obsession that we may end up safe *and* sorry. We understand that these rules are not meant to take the place of thinking but only to give thinking a place to start.

Moreover, such rules often conflict. If it's not broken, don't fix it—but then again, an ounce of prevention is worth a pound of cure. Maybe we're better safe than sorry—but then again, nothing ventured, nothing gained. The moral of the story, once again, is that rules can't replace thinking. They are useful aids, nothing more.

Ethics too has rules. But in ethics, very often we seem to think that the rules somehow are absolute. As with our appeals to authority, we sometimes imagine that appeals to ethical rules can take the place of thinking for ourselves.

For example, the philosopher Immanuel Kant insisted that lying is wrong under all—absolutely all—circumstances. "Tell the truth" is for Kant an absolute rule. According to Kant, even if a murderer in pursuit of an innocent victim comes to you and asks you where his intended victim is, you must answer truthfully. Honesty is not merely the best policy—it is supposed to be the only ethical policy.

Problems with Rules

Once again, however, things are not so clear. In the first place, ethical rules, like all other kinds of rules, have exceptions. Surely Kant was wrong to say that we should never, ever lie. We *should* lie to save an innocent victim. We honor people who sheltered Jews from the Nazis during the 1930s and 1940s in Europe and people who sheltered fugitive slaves from slave owners during the era of slavery in America, even though these acts required systematic deception—nothing so slight as a single lie!—sometimes over a period of many years.

Ethical rules, in reality, are more like familiar nonethical rules of thumb such as "Better safe than sorry." Ethical rules like "Honesty is the best policy" do not tell us what we always must do. They recommend good policies—never claiming that they must be our only policies. ("Never say 'never'? Well, hardly ever . . .") Honesty is a good idea—usually. But the person who insists on following such rules in every circumstance, without question, is the kind of person Mark Twain described as "a good man in the worst sense of the term". We still have to decide.

A second problem with ethical rules is that they con- flict—once again, just like nonethical rules. We must still decide which rule to follow. Jean Valjean, hero of Victor Hugo's *Les Miserables*, was sentenced to hard labor for ten years because he stole a loaf of bread to feed his starving child. Certainly we have a rule that prohibits stealing; it is even one of the Ten Commandments. "Well, then, stealing is always wrong. End of story!" But it is not the end of the story. For Valjean, it is only the beginning. We also have a rule that commands us to protect and nurture our children, and preserving their lives is certainly one of the most basic things we must do. These two rules conflicted; Jean Valjean made a choice.

A third problem concerns those rules that mostly escape the problems of exceptions and conflicts. They escape these problems because they are simply too vague to be useful. The philosopher Jean-Paul Sartre presented the case of a young man in occupied Paris during the Second World War who had to decide between staying with his dependent mother in Paris or escaping to England to fight in the war. Commenting on the decision, Sartre writes:

> Who could help him choose? [The rules that say we should] "be charitable, love your neighbor, take the more rugged path, etc."? But which is the more rugged path? Whom should he love as a [neighbor]? The fighting man or his mother? Which does the greater good, the vague act of fight- ing in a group, or the concrete one of helping a particular human being to go on living?

Sartre's point is that actual decisions, real cases, are too specific for rules to determine. "[Rules] are vague," he says, "and . . . always too broad for the specific and concrete case we are considering." Rules may give us a general orientation, but how to apply them (and, once again, which rule to apply) remains up to us. Once again: in the end, we decide. Not the rules: us.

Consider the Golden Rule, "Do unto others as you would have them do unto you." It is certainly hard to quarrel with the Golden Rule as a general guide to living. But in a way that is just the problem. The Golden Rule is, at best, a general guide to living, not a way to make specific decisions. To say "Do unto others as you would have them do unto you" is really to say: remember that, in the big picture, others are just as real, just as conscious, just as important as yourself. The rule only says: always bear that in mind. Good idea! But the rule does not say anything specific about what we should do. (If a murderer asks you directions, do you tell the truth? Well, if you were the murderer, you'd want the truth. On the other hand, if you were the intended victim . . .) Once again, even with such rules—golden ones, too—you must still think for yourself.

Choosing Is Inescapable

To summarize: whether we admit it or not, we do make our own decisions. We cannot pretend that we are simply obeying some rules (or authorities) that simply settle matters, ours only to obey. In truth, rules have exceptions: you decide when and why. Rules, like authorities, conflict: you decide what to do, which rule to follow. Rules are vague; you decide how to apply them. "Honesty is the best policy"—but it is still up to us to decide when (and how far!) to be honest. "Thou shalt not kill"—but how many of us are pacifists?

The same is true even for nonconformity. As the saying

goes, even nonconformists have to decide what nonconformity to conform to.

Choosing is inescapable. The only thing we accomplish by denying responsibility is that we make it easier for others to manipulate us. The philosopher Bryan Norton relates how his older brother manipulated rules for years to make Bryan do the dishes. If Bryan ate first, his brother cited the rule "Whoever gets the dishes out has to wash them." If his brother ate first, the rule was "Whoever eats last has to wash up." If your attitude toward rules is automatic in this way, like a trusting child's, you are not likely to question someone else's use of rules, and you may end up being exploited—not necessarily so innocently as poor Bryan. Let me say it one last time: think for yourself!

Notes and Comments

Appeals to authority have long been a concern of philosophical ethics, going as far back as Plato's *Euthyphro* (available in many editions, in complete editions of Plato's work, and in partial collections such as the Penguin collection *The Last Days of Socrates*). Here Plato carefully analyzes the relation of the good to the gods and argues that an independent judgment of values is inescapable, even within religious ethics. For a contemporary commentary on and application of Plato's argument, see James Rachels, *The Elements of Moral Philosophy* (New York: McGraw-Hill, 1993), chapter 4.

The same need for independent judgment—in fact, once again, the absolute unavoidability of independent judgment—is a modern theme too. It is crucial, for example, to existentialism. A thorough and engaging philosophical introduction to this theme in existentialism (and its history back through Nietzsche to Kant and earlier) is Frederick Olafson, *Principles and Persons* (Baltimore: Johns

Hopkins University Press, 1967). Joseph Fletcher, in *Situation Ethics* (Philadelphia: Westminster Press, 1974), poses an influential challenge to the appeal to rules, especially in religious ethics, where he calls it "legalism."

Dursi's narration of the My Lai massacre is cited in Howard Zinn, *A People's History of the United States* (NY: HarperCollins, 1980), p. 469.

Here is the prophet Ezekiel interpreting the sin of Sodom: "Behold, this was the guilt of your sister Sodom: she and her daughters had pride, surfeit of food, and prosperous ease, but did not aid the poor and needy" (*Ezekiel* 16:49). On the *Genesis* passage cited in the text, remember that in biblical Hebrew "to know" means to have sexual intercourse. Compare *Genesis* 4:1: "And Adam knew Eve his wife, and she conceived and bore Cain."

On God's willingness to be persuaded by human arguments, see also *Exodus* 32:1–15, where Moses dissuades God from destroying Israel after the incident of the Golden Calf. Here Moses argues with God almost as with an equal. And the Bible explicitly says that, as a result, God "repented of the evil which He thought to do to His people."

Leviticus does explicitly condemn (male) homosexual intercourse (20:13). *Leviticus* also explicitly condemns an extraordinary range of other activities, such as wearing mixed fabrics (19:19), cutting beards (19:27), eating pork or ham (11:7), and harvesting fields right to the edges (19:9–10). Few people take any of these other injunctions seriously. Obviously, once again, we are picking and choosing among rules. Not even an explicit condemnation in the Bible is the end of the story.

Kant's view of rules can be found in his "On a Supposed Right to Lie from Altruistic Motives," in L. W. Beck, ed., *Critique of Practical Reason and Other Writings in Moral Philosophy* (Chicago: University of Chicago Press, 1949). For development of the criticisms made in the text, students might consult Rachels, chapter 9. For philosophers I should note that in rejecting Kant's extremism here, I am not simply presupposing consequentialism. Even modern Kantians reject Kant's view of rules. For discussion of this very case, see Onora Nell, *Acting on Principle* (New York: Columbia University Press, 1975), pp. 133-136. The point is only that in some way, other values besides honesty count too—but *how* they count is still an open question.

The quote from Sartre is from "Existentialism" in *Existentialism and Human Emotions* (New York: Philosophical Library, 1957), p. 25. Bryan Norton tells on his brother in *Toward Unity Among Environmentalists* (NY: Oxford University Press, 1992), p. 238.

¿

3

Finding the Best Problem

—ɯ—

Imagine now that an ethical issue is beginning to emerge: a personal issue about lying or loyalty, or an issue of social justice or environmental preservation, or anything in between. Once any such issue begins to emerge, we are, of course, anxious to begin to resolve it. Life poses a question, a problem: naturally we want an "answer," a "solution."

Experts in problem solving would urge us to take special care at exactly this point. Here is the key: if we are to find the best solutions to our ethical problems, we first need to find the best *problems*. That is, we need to put before ourselves the widest and best range of options, and we need to go to the roots of the problem itself to ask whether there isn't some different and better way in which the problem might come up—if it has to come up at all. In fact, it may be here, before we are even officially look for answers at all, that the greatest promise for creativity in ethics actually lies.

FALSE DILEMMAS

The first step toward "better problems" is to resist thinking that ethical problems somehow must be *dilemmas.* Sometimes perhaps they are, but less often than we usually think.

Remember Kant's hypothetical example: if a murderer came to the door asking which way his intended victim went, would you lie or tell the truth? Supposedly the choice is simply to lie or not to lie. We are never encouraged to look for any other options. But now suppose that we did look. There is a wonderful story about Saint Athanasius, pursued by persecutors who intended to kill him, trying to escape by rowing along a river. Along came his pursuers, furiously rowing in the other direction. "Where is the traitor Athanasius?" they cried. "Not far away" replied the saint and rowed right by, unsuspected.

One could argue a long time about whether or not Athanasius actually lied. In any case he did not lie outright. Literally, he told the exact truth. Perhaps Kant would still not approve. My point, however, is that Kant overlooked a few things. Outright lies are not the only way to lie, and telling the whole truth is not the only way to tell the truth. Athanasius seems to have been a little more imaginative.

Sartre's Young Man

One of the most famous examples in ethical philosophy is a dilemma described by the French philosopher Jean-Paul Sartre and briefly mentioned in the last chapter. A young man in occupied Paris during World War Two came to Sartre for advice.

His father was on bad terms with his mother, and, moreover, was inclined to be a collaborationist [i.e., he cooperated with the Nazis]; his older brother had been killed in the German offensive of 1940, and the young man, with somewhat immature but generous feelings, wanted to avenge him. His mother lived alone with him, very much upset by the half-treason of her husband and the death of her elder son; the boy was her only consolation.

The boy was faced with the choice of leaving for England and joining the Free French forces—that is, leaving his mother behind—or remaining with his mother and helping her to carry on. He was fully aware that the woman lived only for him and that his going-off—and perhaps his death—would plunge her into despair. He was also aware that every act that he did for his mother's sake was a sure thing, in the sense that it was helping her to carry on, whereas every effort he made toward going off and fighting was an uncertain move which might run aground and prove completely useless. . . . He was faced with two very different kinds of action: one concrete, immediate, but concerning only one individual; the other concerned an incomparably vaster group, a national collectivity, but for that very reason was dubious, and might be interrupted en route. . . .

What should the young man do? Imagine that he came to you for advice in this situation. What would you say?

Sartre did not answer the young man in the way we might expect. He did not tell the young man what to do. Instead, Sartre wanted the young man to recognize that the choice was his—that neither Sartre, nor anyone else, nor any rule could make the choice for him—and that he was free to do anything. "I had only one answer to give: 'You're free, choose, that is, invent.'" Sartre bases a whole ethical doctrine on such a claim: he argues that ethical choices shape our selves, rather than vice versa. Our choices have no basis because only in choosing do we, in effect, create their basis.

So Sartre is using this case to make a philosophical point. In the specific and face-to-face situation, however, he fails the young man, and in a remarkable and striking way that few of the many commentators on this story have noticed. This is the problem: Sartre takes it for granted that the young man has only two, sharply different and totally opposed options. He takes it for granted that the young man really does face a dilemma. He never asks whether there are any other or better options. But, once again, there probably are.

Why couldn't the young man stay with his mother long enough to wean her from her (alleged) dependence, for instance, and then head for England? The war will last for a while; he's not likely to miss it. Why couldn't he work for the Free French in Paris—spying or sabotaging? Dangerous work, to be sure, but then so is heading across occupied territory to England in order to turn around and fight on the front lines.

And even this is still only the crudest and most obvious level on which to work. Any good counselor would ask much more. Must the situation itself be accepted as given? Is the father a completely lost cause? Could Sartre help the young man explore what Sartre himself calls the "immaturity" of his demand for revenge? Is the mother really so graspingly dependent, or is she perhaps capable of a little patriotism and independence too? Has the son even asked her what she wants?

Sartre never explores any of these questions. Both he and the young man seem far too ready to assume that the situation is set in stone. It looks like a real dilemma, but in fact it isn't. It is, instead, a false dilemma.

The Heinz Dilemma

Consider another famous ethical dilemma, this time from the psychologist Lawrence Kohlberg's research on moral development.

A woman was near death from cancer. One drug might save her, a form of radium that a druggist in the same town had discovered. The druggist was charging $2000, ten times what the drug cost him to make. The sick woman's husband, Heinz, went to everyone he knew to borrow the money, but he could only get together about half of what it cost. He told the druggist that his wife was dying and asked him to sell it cheaper or let him pay later. But the druggist said "no." The husband got desperate and broke into the man's store to steal the drug for his wife. Should the husband have done that? Why?

Kohlberg used this and similar dilemmas to probe children's moral reasoning. He found that children go through several markedly different stages of moral reasoning, and that these stages tend to be the same for most children. His theory has proven fascinating and controversial, setting off one of the biggest debates and ongoing research projects in contemporary psychology and ethics.

But that is not our concern here. Let us ask just this: Is this a true dilemma or a false one? Does Heinz really have no options besides stealing the drug or watching his wife die?

I put this question to my introductory ethics classes after they get a little training in problem solving. Can they think of any other options for Heinz? It turns out that they can—easily. Here are some of their ideas.

For one thing, Heinz might offer the druggist something besides money. Perhaps he has some skill that the druggist could use: maybe he's a good house painter or piano tuner or skilled chemist. He could barter, trading the use of his skills for the drug.

For another thing, some form of public or charitable assistance is probably available. Almost every society in which modern medicine is available has developed some way of offering it to people who cannot afford it themselves. Heinz should at least investigate.

Or suppose Heinz called up a newspaper. Nothing like a little bad publicity to change the druggist's mind. Publicity might also help the sick woman gain a few donations. A thousand dollars—all that she needs—is not a lot of money in today's world.

And why is the druggist so inflexible, anyway? Possibly he needs the money to promote or keep on developing his drug. But in that case Heinz could argue that a spectacular cure would be the best promotion of all. Maybe his wife should get it free. Or Heinz could buy half of the drug with the money he can raise and then—if it works—ask for the rest to complete the demonstration.

And again: why we should trust the "miracle drug" in the first place is not clear. New lifesaving drugs require extensive testing, which evidently has not happened yet in this case. Maybe the drug is not worth taking even if the sick woman could get it free. Or maybe she should be paid to participate in a drug test!

So Heinz does have a few options. There are more possibilities to choose from besides trying to steal the drug or letting his wife die. This is only a partial list, too. I am constantly delighted by students' ability to come up with new ideas.

I don't mean that there are no ethical issues raised by the dilemma itself as Kohlberg states it. There are. And of course (I add this point for philosophers), if one's goal in raising this dilemma is to illustrate the clash of certain ethical theories, then it can easily be altered to foreclose some of the other options. Certainly some situations really are dilemmas. My point, however, is that we are all too ready to accept purported ethical dilemmas without question, as if somehow dilemmas are the only appropriate or natural form for ethical problems. We foreclose the possibility of creative thinking before we even start. We pose narrow and limited questions that leave us, not surprisingly, with narrow and limited answers.

HOW TO EXPAND YOUR OPTIONS

Faced with a problem, then, our question is: how do we expand our options? How do we come up with new ideas?

Here is one method, probably the most obvious, and for that very reason the most commonly overlooked. *Ask around*. Listening to other people is not a bad idea anyway, and here it is crucial. There's no telling what other people may know.

Probably you have seen pictures of the huge, mysterious stone monoliths of Easter Island: vaguely human-like statues made of enormous carved stones, some of them weighing almost fifty tons, somehow carved and then assembled by a scattered tribal people with no developed machinery at all. How could they have built such statues? Some popular writers have argued that they simply couldn't, and therefore that the statues must have been built by some ancient, alien astronauts who visited Earth to set off the process of civilization.

A more reasonable conclusion would be that there probably is some stone-raising method we just haven't thought of. The explorer Thor Heyerdahl learned of one method by —you guessed it—asking a few of the island's natives. He simply offered to pay them $100 to raise one of the fallen blocks. They set right to work, prying it up with long poles and wedging small stones in the cracks that were created. Then they added larger stones, then more little ones on top, then larger ones, and so on. Eventually they raised a thirty-ton block twelve feet and slid it neatly into place. They knew how; it turned out that they had been taught the old ways from birth (in fact, literally from birth: in lullabyes, for example). Until Heyerdahl, though, no one had bothered to ask them. Previous explorers and scientists were so confident of the superiority of their civilization, I suppose, that they could not imagine native peoples, with a few sticks and stones, accomplishing a task that modern technologies would find difficult.

A little psychology is useful here. Our thinking is often limited by habits and unconscious assumptions that worked well for us in the past. Psychologists use the word "set" to describe these habits and assumptions. (They're like concrete: at first they're fluid, but they quickly "set" and then we can't move.) Set can be so powerful that we literally cannot see any other options, even those right before our eyes.

Here, for a quick illustration, is a little riddle. A worker at a large factory leaves work every night pushing a wheelbarrow full of garbage. Theft is a problem at the plant, so every night the garbage is carefully inspected. Nothing is ever found. Yet the thefts continue. Question: What is the worker stealing?

Stop and think about it for a moment.

The answer is: wheelbarrows. Perfectly obvious, isn't it? But many people never solve this riddle at all. Usually, like the guard, we fixate entirely on what is *in* the wheelbarrow, so we simply do not notice the wheelbarrow itself. We assume that what is being stolen must be hidden, buried in the garbage, and so we miss what rolls right by us in broad daylight.

Understanding "set" helps us appreciate some of the more unusual methods for expanding our options. We need to loosen up, try something new—maybe even something that seems peculiar, embarrassing, or improbable. It may feel forced, but that's just the point: you're trying to force your way beyond your own habits.

For example, problem-solving expert Edward De Bono proposes a method he calls the "intermediate impossible." If you have a problem, start by imagining what would be the perfect solution. Presumably the absolutely perfect solution will be impossible. Then, however, work backward toward intermediate solutions that *are* possible, until you find a possibility that is realistic. In short, make your very first step a big, wild one; otherwise you may never take a big step at all.

"Brainstorming" is another good method. Brainstorming is a process in which a group of people try to generate new ideas. The key rule is: defer criticism. It is tempting and safe to react to any new suggestion with criticism. Brainstorming asks us to do just the opposite: to consider how some new idea *could* work, not why it probably won't. Even a crude and obviously unrealistic idea, passed around the room, may evolve into something much more realistic. Meanwhile it may spark other new ideas too. Ideas hitchhike on each other. Let it happen.

One further rule often used in brainstorming is that quantity is important. Some groups set quotas for new ideas and allow no criticism until the quota is met. This also helps new ideas to percolate and gives people room to think in an exploratory way, free from the fear of being criticized.

If you're still stumped, De Bono has another, truly wild suggestion. Go to the dictionary, or to any book for that matter. Open it to any page and choose a word at random. Any word will do. Then see what associations that word suggests. The point is: immediately your thinking has a truly new stimulus. You are not just going around in the same old circles. De Bono calls this method "random association."

Once again it may seem silly. Once again, though, some such stimulus may be just what we need in order to break our set. You will still need to work on the new ideas once you've found them, but random association is a wonderful way of generating them.

You can practice, too. Most of us have been asked, in some game or quiz-book setting, how many new and different uses we can think of for some everyday object, like a brick. I do this with my ethics students too: it helps them get in shape for ethical problems like the famous but false dilemmas with which this chapter began. So what can you do with a brick, besides build a house? Obviously, it can be a paperweight or a doorstop. You can make bookcases out of bricks and wood. OK, I say, but can you be more creative still? J. L. Adams, using this example in his book *Conceptual Blockbusting,* suggests a new track event: the "brick put," by analogy to the shot put. Or suppose you tape on a return-postage-guaranteed junk mail reply envelope and drop your brick in a mailbox—a good way to protest junk mail. Suppose you leave it in your yard until you want to go fishing and then lift it up to collect the worms underneath. (This last suggestion is courtesy of one of my students. Brick as "worm generator," he called it.) There is no end of novel functions!

And that's the moral of the story. Confronted with two or three bad choices and the demand to make a decision, start brainstorming. Free-associate. Ask around. Don't let anyone tell you that you have no other options. Maybe you don't, maybe you do, but you will not find out until you start looking for them.

HOW TO REFRAME PROBLEMS

So far, I have pointed out that our alleged ethical dilemmas (and limited choices in general) can be expanded by generating new options. But a more radical approach is also often possible. There is a particular kind of set I call "freezing the problem." We freeze a problem when we act as though all we can do is to cope with the problem, accomodate ourselves to it, react after it has happened. Suppose, though, that the problem itself can be changed, made less serious, or even eliminated. The key question might be: why not try to prevent the problem from even coming up? What about thinking preventively, so that in the end there is no problem at all?

Consider first an example that does not involve ethical issues. Some friends of mine loved to have fires in their fireplace. But they lived in a house so designed that when they wanted to use the fireplace, they had to haul firewood through nearly the whole house to get it there. The result was that they seldom built fires, and when they did they made a huge mess. For years they just tried to carry wood more carefully. Later they hauled wood in a box. But this was awkward too. The halls were still small, the box large.

What would you suggest? No doubt there are still more creative options: cutting wood into really tiny pieces, or buying the dirt-free fake logs sold in hardware stores, or getting some nice dirt-colored carpet so the mess is less noticeable. Once again, however, notice that all of these ideas leave the problem as it is. They freeze the problem rather than change it. Suppose that instead we ask: is there a way to prevent this problem from even coming up?

Here is what a precocious cousin finally proposed: knock a hole in the wall right next to the fireplace and put in a little door and a woodbox. My friends were delighted and did just that. Voilà—end of problem!

My friends missed an obvious and simple alternative because they were preoccupied with better ways to haul wood through the house. They were becoming very good at accommodating themselves to a badly designed house, when in fact they needed to change the house.

So, odd as it may sound, solving problems is not the only way to deal with them. Sometimes it is not even the best way. Notice that my friends did not actually solve the problem of how to haul wood through the house without making a mess. They simply eliminated that problem. Now they don't haul wood through the house at all. There is no problem left to solve.

Preventive Ethics

Faced with an ethical problem or dilemma, then, one question we need to ask is: can the problem itself be changed, made less serious, or even eliminated? We need to look at the bigger picture, at the causes of problems, and ask what we can do about *them*.

Kohlberg has us worry about whether or not Heinz should steal a drug that is necessary to save his dying wife. Or maybe Heinz can find some other way to save his wife or get the drug. But there is a range of more probing background questions that he does not ask. For example, why does the sick woman have no insurance? Why can't public assistance help her? If either insurance or public assistance were real options, Heinz's dilemma would not come up in the first place.

We have learned to ask what should be done when the family of a person in a "persistent vegetative state" wants her respirator turned off. Now let us learn to ask the background questions, like why nobody knows her wishes on the subject, or why the hospital's lawyers have the last word, or why she is in the hospital (as opposed for example, to a hospice or at home, where the family has the last word) to begin with. Why not mandate much clearer "living wills" (a person's declaration about what she wishes done should she become comatose, made while still of sound mind)? Why not take end-state care out of hospitals entirely?

Executives and managers worry about whether whistle blowers are being disloyal or destructive, while consumer advocates worry about how to encourage and protect them. But what about the preventive questions? How could the need for whistle blowing be prevented in the first place? Some reformers propose much more effective ways of protecting lines of communication and complaint within corporations and bureaucracies, thereby reducing or eliminating the need to go public with disruptive and controversial accusations, ruining one's own professional life and possibly those of others along the way. Others have suggested more effective public participation in large corporations, so that abuses become less frequent. Some experiments along these lines have been tried. We need to pay more attention. The possibility of such reforms is every bit as much an answer to the problem of whistle blowing as the usual hand wringing about the conflicting values of loyalty and honesty and such. Why let such conflicts become so intense in the first place?

We worry about "the drug problem." But all we usually see are offenders—dealers and users—and all we usually consider is punishment: jail, mandatory sentencing, more police. In fact, a whole range of constructive possibilities is being ignored. There are truly fundamental questions here, like why people are attracted to drugs in the first place, and why it is so difficult to get free later. Surely part of the appeal of drugs, at least initially, is that they offer some excitement in the midst of an otherwise uninteresting life. Then one bottom-line question is: are there less lethal ways to make life more interesting? Yes, obviously. Well, what ways?

Now there's a fine question! What can we do to make life so interesting that people are no longer tempted to escape through drugs? A truly better problem: no longer punitive, widely engaging, promising for all of us.

Of course, problems cannot always be reframed. Sometimes there is no time. Heinz, for example, may have very few options left. A person on a respirator in a hospital is already thoroughly "framed." There may be some ethical questions that cannot usefully be reframed even if there is time. The strategies suggested here will not always yield happy solutions. The point, though, is that we tend to overlook even the *possibility* of reframing our problems. We must not simply assume that reframing is impossible and condemn ourselves to just bearing up under our dilemmas.

The Abortion Debate

So far I have said very little about the abortion debate, partly because it is one of the most acrimonious and seemingly hopeless debates we have at present. Surely it is a frozen problem if any problem is. Many people are also frozen into their positions. Almost no one asks if there are ways to change things so that the abortion problem in its present form simply doesn't come up at all, or comes up in more manageable and less divisive forms. We completely resign ourselves to it. Is reframing possible even with a problem such as this?

Let us ask the kinds of preventive questions just illustrated. The demand for abortion arises in cases of unintended and/or unwanted pregnancy. Already, then, we can ask a somewhat different question from the usual ones. Our question will be: how can we prevent or reduce the demand for abortions themselves? Is there any realistic way to prevent the number of unwanted pregnancies and/or keep those unintended pregnancies that do occur from being unwanted?

Recent figures show that half of all women who seek abortions used no contraception. Why? We need to find out. Lack of access? Lack of support? Lack of education? These things can be changed. Changing them might not even be that controversial. Even the Catholic church endorses some forms of contraception.

And what about the other half, women who used contraception and still got pregnant? Again, we need to find out why. Poor or difficult-to-use methods? Resistance from male spouses and lovers? But these things too can be changed. With a fraction of the energy and intensity put into the present abortion debate, they *could* be changed.

If we are to reduce the demand for abortions, we must also understand why pregnancy, or pregnancy at the wrong time, is so unacceptably burdensome for so many women. Another statistic is revealing: over 80 percent of American women seeking abortions are unmarried, and most are either working, attending school, or both. There's part of the answer: they can't *afford* a child or another child. Not in a society in which most women still earn much less than comparably skilled men, in which most of the work of child raising is still left to mothers, in which pregnancy and maternity leaves from work are still grudgingly available at best, and in which affordable and reliable child care is difficult to find. Those are the realities behind the abortion rates.

They are also things that can be changed. Economic justice for women is, or ought to be, a goal of our whole society. Shared child raising has everything to recommend it.

Paid parental leaves are the norm in Europe. These things are achievable here; what we need, again, are some of the attention and energy currently being wasted on endless confrontations at abortion clinics. We could even argue for some reconstructive measures—community support for affordable child care, for example—as a way of helping to break the deadlock over abortion.

In fact, it has already begun to happen. In 1985 a Wisconsin state legislator, weary of the endless deadlocked debate, organized a committee of legislators and activists from the opposed sides with the aim of cooperating, as far as possible, to identify shared goals and to draft legislation to promote them. A shocking thought! Even more shocking is that they succeeded. The resulting bill passed the legislature—unanimously. Among other things, it provides money for sex education and pregnancy counseling, with the hope of reducing unintended pregnancies, and for a state adoption center and hotline to make adoption a more realistic alternative. Both sides got much of what they wanted, and along the way each side also acknowledged that much of what the other side wanted is not such a bad idea.

Constructive change is possible. We only have to ask the right questions. Perhaps the time is now.

Of course, the old questions remain too. We can—and sometimes must—also debate about whether abortion itself (or euthanasia, whistle blowing, etc.) is right or wrong. The point here, once again, is that these are not the only questions to ask. And often they are not the best questions either. Ethics needn't just be a reactive business. There is no reason to resign ourselves to the problems as they are. Don't pick the lesser of two evils. Try to pick *no* evils: try, if you can, to change the problem.

Notes and Comments

"False dilemma" is a classic fallacy in informal logic and is usefully discussed and illustrated in many informal logic textbooks, such as Howard Kahane's *Logic and Contemporary Rhetoric* (Belmont, CA: Wadsworth).

Creative methods of generating new options are also discussed widely, but most of this discussion takes place in literatures unfamiliar to philosophers, such as the problem solving literature in management and design. For an introduction to problem solving broadly conceived, see Marvin Levine, *Effective Problem Solving* (Englewood Cliffs, NJ: Prentice-Hall, 1988) and the many works of Edward de Bono, such as *Lateral Thinking* (New York: Harper and Row, 1970).

De Bono describes what he calls "PO thinking": PO for hyPOthesis, POssible, POetry and short for "Provocative Operation." The opposite of PO is NO, as in "No way!" Confronted with a dilemma, we say "No way!": we think there is no way out. De Bono urges us to say instead "PO way!": maybe there are ways. Methods like brainstorming and random word association are intended precisely to be "provocative operations" in the service of finding them.

As I say in the text, one can certainly redescribe the Heinz dilemma or other examples to cut off each new option as it comes up, so that finally Heinz, like Sartre's young man, must "just choose." If your purpose is solely to illustrate the clash of different ethical theories, this may seem to be a natural move, and trying to come up with new options may indeed seem to confuse things, even to miss the point. And of course, as the text emphasizes too, there *are* genuinely hard choices.

Nonetheless, there are often other options too. From a practical point of view, even a few problem-solving skills go a long way. We need the encouragement to look for other options, to avoid locking ourselves into unpromising problems.

From a philosophical point of view, moreover, the possibility of creatively rethinking ethical problems raises the question of the very nature of ethical problems. If ethical problems are like puzzles, distinct and well defined, then trying to rethink the problems themselves does miss the point. The problems exist to be solved. But *are* ethical problems like puzzles? The philosopher John Dewey argues that ethical problems are more like large, vague regions of tension, not at all distinct or well defined. No "solution" can really be expected. Ethical problems are also, for the same reason, regions of opportunity. Constructively engaging the problem, trying to change it into something more manageable, is the most intelligent response—often the only intelligent response.

Let me put this another way. The Heinz dilemma and its cousins offer themselves as "real life." That is why the clash of ethical theories that they are typically used to illustrate is supposed to be so important. But does real life really consist of dilemmas? Is the clash of ethical theories so crucially important? Let us at least look around and ask. We beg the question if we just assume that this or any ethical problem is necessarily a dilemma, and therefore doctor all of our examples to make it seem so. When we manage to avoid begging the question this way, I think it is pretty clear that our most troublesome ethical problems are much more like what Dewey called "problematic situations" than like puzzles.

For further discussion of these points and an extended argument for the last claim, see my book *Toward Better Problems* (Philadelphia: Temple University Press, 1992). For Dewey's view, see James Gouinlock's collection *The Moral Writings of John Dewey* (New York: Hafner-Macmillan, 1976). Philosophical readers should also explore the many suggestive feminist approaches outlined in the *Hypatia* 4 (1989) volume on feminist medical ethics. See also my article "Toward a Social Critique of Bioethics," *Journal of Social Philosophy* 12 (1991), pp. 109-118.

The Athanasius story comes from Peter Geach, *The Virtues* (Cambridge: Cambridge University Press, 1977), p. 114.

The Sartre quotation is from "Existentialism," in *Existentialism and Human Emotions* (New York: Philosophical Library, 1957), pp. 24-25.

The Heinz dilemma is cited from Lawrence Kohlberg, "Stage and Sequence: the Cognitive-Developmental Approach to Socialization," in D. A. Goslin, ed., *Handbook of Socialization Theory and Research* (Chicago: Rand McNally, 1969), p. 379. For a critique of Kohlberg's conclusions, see Carol Gilligan, *In a Different Voice* (Cambridge, MA: Harvard University Press, 1983), pp. 27-38. There is an extended discussion of the Kohlberg–Gilligan debate in Eva Kittay and Diana Meyers, eds., *Women and Moral Theory* (Totowa, NJ: Rowman and Littlefield, 1986).

Astonishingly enough, subjects in Kohlberg's studies were graded as morally "immature" if they started exploring other possible options for Heinz. The researchers concluded that these subjects just didn't understand the dilemma. In fact, I think, they understood it better than the researchers. They understood it as a false dilemma, which is exactly what it is.

The term "preventive ethics" is Virginia Warren's: see her essay "Feminist Directions in Medical Ethics," *Hypatia* 4 (1989), pp. 73-78, and my discussion in *Toward Better Problems*, pp. vii-viii, 24-28, and 183.

On whistle blowing, see any recent anthology in business ethics, such as Tom Beauchamp and Norman Bowie, eds, *Ethical Theory and Business*, 3rd ed. (Englewood Cliffs, NJ: Prentice-Hall, 1993), chapter 5. On "pulling the plug," see any recent bioethics anthology or casebook, such as Thomas Mappes and Jane Zembaty, eds., *Biomedical Ethics*, 3rd ed. (New York: McGraw-Hill, 1987).

More on the possible reconstruction of the abortion debate can be found in my *Toward Better Problems*, pp. 60-68. The data cited on p. 43 on contraceptive use come from Natalie Angier, "Future of the Pill May Lie Just Over the Counter," *New York Times*, August 8, 1993, p. E5. The same article reports that two-thirds of all pregnancies in America each year are unintended. Half of these end in abortion. The data cited on p. 43 about how many American women seeking abortions are married, working, and so on comes from Rosalind Petchesky, "Abortion Politics in the 90s," *The Nation* 250:1 (May 28, 1990), p. 732. On the Wisconsin legislation mentioned on p. 44, see Beth Maschinot, "Compromising Positions," *In These Times* 10:3 (November 20-26, 1985), p. 4.

4

When Values Conflict

—ɯ—

Most ethical questions arise because values conflict. Our
own values often conflict with each other, or conflict with
the values of other people with whom we must reach some
sort of agreement. Sometimes these are the same conflicts:
our conflicting inner voices may sound a lot like the conflicting voices outside us.

From a practical point of view, one of the key tasks of
ethics is to resolve such conflicts. It is not easy. There is no
guarantee that our usual ways of approaching conflicts will
produce constructive results. Possibly they even drag us in
the other direction. Here too, it turns out, there is a lot of
room for improvement. Here too ethics can help.

POLARIZING VALUES

On many major ethical issues, there are usually supposed to be just two clearly distinct and opposite positions. The most obvious and painful example is the abortion debate. "Pro-life" and "pro-choice" positions are set against each other, and no other options are even discussed. No ambiguity, no gray areas, no middle ground. Values are *polarized*.

Polarization has two aspects. First, we imagine two and only two possibilities, and these are almost always, as in the abortion debate, fairly extreme. Values are simplified and reduced. In debates about environmentalism, to take another example, it is common for any kind of environmentalism to be called "misanthropic" (that is, against human values), while environmentalists, for their part, often portray their opponents as short-sighted, narrow-minded vandals. Likewise, the media regularly approach environmental issues in terms of "environment versus jobs" or, in the case of one famous *Time* magazine cover, "Owl versus Man" (about the standoff between timber interests and endangered spotted owls in the Pacific Northwest).

Moreover, we tend to suppose that one side—our own side, of course!—is completely right and the other side is completely wrong. This is the second aspect of polarization. The polarizations we imagine are not neutral. We polarize values precisely in order to be able to picture ourselves as totally justified, totally right, and the "other side" as totally unjustified and wrong. All good on one side, all evil on the other. Day and night, black and white, us and them. We represent goodness and light; the other side, whatever it is, represents darkness and unfathomable evil. Polarizing values therefore makes things crystal clear, protects us from doubts, and justifies us completely. The battle lines become clear. There are obvious and irredeemable enemies. Our choices become easy.

Look at the bumper stickers next time you drive. "Pro-choice is pro-death" says one in my neighborhood. The response—two blocks over—is "'Pro-life' isn't." Pro-lifers routinely condemn the other side as selfish baby killers. Pro-choicers return the favor by painting the other side as some kind of woman-hating, repressive, Bible-thumping fanatics. Extremists from one side have been known to applaud aborted fetuses, while those on the other side are barely able to express ritual regret at the murders of doctors at women's centers.

Look at the labeling that goes on all around us. The civil rights movement, the women's movement, and in fact nearly every progressive social movement since the 1930s were written off as "Communist," usually with little or no understanding of communism itself. (These days, to call someone a Communist is often a joke, but for a long time it was deadly serious.) Liberals may return the favor by labeling conservative social movements "Nazi" (or "fascist"). Neither word really means anything in these debates. Their function is only to evoke the images of darkness and evil that keep us from having to think more carefully.

Every political campaign, meanwhile, seems designed to polarize us. Each side works up its own frenzy by radically simplifying, if not completely misrepresenting, the other side's views, and then attacking and condemning them. Go to any campaign rally and it will be unclear to you why anyone could ever in good conscience vote for the other side. Yet, oddly enough, people do.

CAN BOTH SIDES BE RIGHT?

"But doesn't the world really come in opposites?" someone may ask. "Isn't that just the way things are?"

Is it? We sometimes picture the world as coming in

opposites, like day and night, hard and soft, hot and cold. But these are just our pictures, not the world. Hot and cold? No specific temperature has an opposite: there are just other temperatures. You and me? We are distinct but not opposite. From the point of view of an amoeba or a Martian, we are much more alike than different—and besides, there are other people too. Day and night, dark and light? Painters identify hundreds of different qualities of light, nothing so crude as "day" and "night." Cycles of light and dark, each of varying quality (sunny days, rainy days, moonlit nights, storms) follow each other, like the seasons, with no clear dividing lines. When does the day begin? The sky is light long before the sun rises. Besides, the real world comes in *color:* neither blacks nor whites nor grays.

Similarly, in nearly every serious ethical issue, the truth is that both sides have a point. Or rather, all sides have a point, since there are usually more than two. All sides speak for something worth considering.

Consider how different the abortion debate looks, for example, if we ask not which (one) side is right but what *each* side is right *about.* Suppose, in short, that we finally acknowledge that *both* of the basic contending values—fetal life and pregnant women's autonomy—matter, and matter profoundly.

Fetal life matters, in the first place, even if the fetus is not a full-fledged human being. We recognize this every time we mourn a miscarriage. We are even beginning to take seriously the life possibilities of creatures that are not human. Surely we ought to have at least some care for fetuses. There's another bumper sticker—this one a lot better than the usual slogans—that asks: why do we brake for animals and save the whales but have no problem with abortion? The question has answers, but it is a good question.

On the other side, we value autonomy strongly too. The

right to control what happens in and to our own bodies is one of our most basic values. Even most abortion opponents acknowledge this in some form, which is the reason pregnancies caused by rape are often considered exceptions to otherwise strict antiabortion laws. Fetuses are no different whether conceived by rape or not, yet here we almost all acknowledge that something else also matters—and may even matter more than the fetus's right to life.

Except when we are in the midst of the abortion debate, in fact, the value of autonomy is axiomatic. We are fanatical about our freedoms. Many Americans still object even to the minor inconvenience of mandatory seat belts. Yet a seat belt is nothing compared to a pregnancy.

It is one sign of how polarized the abortion debate has become that even these very simple points are likely to seem suspicious to one side or the other. We have trouble acknowledging that there is *any* sense on the other side, that fetal life or women's autonomy matter at all. But they do—both of them. The issue arises in the first place, and won't go away, because both sides are, in this sense, right.

It is a mistake, then, to insist that only one side is right and the other is just wrong. It is also a mistake to insist that there are just two sides, that there are just two relevant values at stake in the first place. In truth, there usually are other values also at stake besides the official two.

For example, imagine a fetus that, if carried to term, will be born severely retarded or with fatal physical defects. This raises issues different from either women's rights or fetal rights: it raises quality-of-life issues. National polls consistently show that the prospect of such a degraded quality of life is considered a sufficient reason for abortion by most people, even by many who otherwise oppose abortion. But it's not exactly consistent, especially with right-to-life arguments, because the quality of life should not make a difference to one's right to it. Some people, of course, do oppose all abortions, even in rape or incest cases, even when the resultant child will suffer only a short and unremittingly painful life. The very fact that this is such an extreme view, however, makes the point. Realistically, there are other values at stake, and most of us know it.

Right versus Right

As another example, consider the "owl versus man" face-off once again. Here too, let us not ask which side is right, but rather what *each* side is right *about.* It should come as no surprise, once we look at the issue calmly and carefully, that both sides are speaking for something important.

Preserving ancient species (and their old-growth forest habitat) is important for its own sake: we respect their antiquity. Their beauty is important. Their possible contribution to environmental health (a contribution that we still barely understand) is important, not least because our own fate too depends upon it. We may even have the vague feeling that the possibility of our own lives being rich and rewarding partly depends upon a richly varied natural world.

On the other hand, we care about preserving people's jobs and the communities that depend on the timber economy. We care about the quality of life that timber products make possible. We care about the health of local and global economies and the quality of life that depends upon it. We don't want a world in which no tree is ever cut down no matter what.

We know these things. We can finally acknowledge all of them, too, once we recognize that it is not a matter of one side being completely right and the other completely wrong. In short, in environmental questions as in the abortion debate, we have an ethical issue precisely because we have conflicts between different things, perhaps incompatible things, that are good. The real story is not good versus evil, but good versus good. Not right versus wrong, but right versus right.

"Only dogmatism," says John Dewey, "can suppose that serious moral conflict is between something clearly bad and something known to be good, and that uncertainty lies wholly in the will of the one choosing. Most conflicts of importance are conflicts between things which are or have been satisfying, not between good and evil." It is time to move past polarized values.

One Qualification

Dewey speaks carefully. He says "*most*": "most conflicts of importance are conflicts between things which are or have been satisfying, not between good and evil" (my emphasis). It is *usually* true that each side is right about something, and looking for it is certainly better than assuming that only one side has all the answers. Still, some issues really do reduce to right versus wrong. There are truly evil things in this world, and we need to be able to reject them unequivocally. The point is only that these cases are probably fewer than we think.

In fact, even when we are confronted with an evil viewpoint, it is still essential to pay attention to its advocates. Not because we agree with them, but in order to ask why the evil is so attractive. To see, that is, if the *people* can be saved from the *position*. For example, fanaticism may sometimes arise out of a profound sense of insecurity. Hatred against "outside" groups may arise out of a deep sense of exclusion and disempowerment. And this too, before it settles on some scapegoat, could be a perfectly valid feeling. Just repressing the hateful ones leaves the attraction of the hate itself untouched. Repression may even drive it deeper, making it more attractive. Even here, then—even when we can genuinely speak of right versus wrong—we need to try to listen, to try to figure out the other side rather than just condemning it outright, and to try to figure out how the people attracted to it can be reached.

INTEGRATING VALUES

Clearly we need a different way of approaching conflicts of values besides the winner-take-all, fight-to-the-death approach so common now. When right conflicts with right, how should we decide? Where do we go from here?

The answer is that we need to try to *integrate* or *harmonize* the values at stake. If both sides (or all sides) are to some extent right, then we need to try to honor what is right in each of them. We need to take account of all of the important values at stake, rather than just a few.

This is a lot less mysterious than it may sound. In fact, we do something of the sort constantly. Almost every important choice in our lives is made in the face of the need to integrate values. Let me begin with a simple, nonethical example.

Suppose that, for our summer vacation, you want to go to the beach and I want to go to the mountains. We could just battle it out, or flip a coin, and end up doing one or the other. A better way would be to compromise: maybe this year the beach, next year the mountains. Or maybe we could do a little of each this year. Though compromising is sometimes treated as disgraceful or weak-willed, here it seems to be quite the opposite: a clear-headed acknowledgment of the diversity of values at stake and an attempt to answer at least partly to both of them. Simple.

But perhaps we can do better still. Suppose that you and

I try to figure out *why* we want to go to the beach or the mountains. Maybe it turns out that you want to be able to swim and sunbathe, and I want to be able to hike. These goals are not incompatible at all. There are some great lakes in the mountains and some great hiking trails near the ocean. Both of us can have exactly, or almost exactly, what we want, and at the same time too.

This is what I mean by integrating values. Like the methods discussed in the previous chapter, integrating values calls upon problem-solving skills: generating new options and reframing problems. Here, however, the emphasis is upon values. We are concerned to identify the compatibility of seemingly incompatible values, to find ways to achieve or to honor both (all) of them. It is not always possible, of course: sometimes good things really are incompatible. However, we have no business assuming that they are incompatible, in any given problematic situation, until we've taken the care to look.

Take "Owl versus Man." I have argued that both sides are speaking for things that are important. Ideally, we would have both old-growth forests *and* jobs. We could, of course, try to compromise, to maintain at least some of both. This is not irresponsible or morally weak, especially if done well. Since so little old growth is left, for example, the health of the timber industry hardly depends upon it; perhaps no more needs to be cut at all. Other, less ecologically and aesthetically valuable places could be cut instead.

Once again, though, we should be able to do better still. There may be more integrative possibilities. If we could create jobs based on owl-watching tourism, for instance, as has been done successfully with whales, then owl interests and human interests would converge rather than diverge. We would truly harmonize values. Or again, we could seek to create a sustainable timber industry, using wood in a more intensive, craft-based way rather than shipping massive amounts of raw wood abroad or pulping it for plywood, as the timber corporations do at present. That kind of logging, unlike the present practice, would have a future: better for loggers *and* the forests.

In the current lingo, this would be a "win-win" solution. Instead of one side winning everything and the other side losing everything, both sides could gain. Indeed they would no longer appear to be opposite sides at all. Stephen Covey, writing of the Buddhist search for the so-called "middle way," says: "'Middle' in this sense does not mean compromise: it means higher, like the apex of a triangle." When right clashes with right, we are called to just such a search for something "higher": something that honors the values on both (or, rather, all) sides, something that allows us to go on together, something that encourages creative new strategies—integrative solutions.

Even in the abortion debate, it turns out, integrative solutions are possible. I can hardly think of a better recommendation for them.

We might, for starters, try compromise. Notice that although two important values are at stake in this debate, they are not at stake at the same moment in the same way. Autonomy could be honored first; then, as the fetus matures, the balance could swing in the other direction. Suppose that we allow abortions early in pregnancy, when the embryo is barely developed and the pregnant woman's autonomy can be most readily and safely exercised. Suppose that we also prohibit abortions (or most of them—there will still be some exceptions) once the fetus is more developed and has more of a claim and autonomy has, so to speak, been given its chance. Suppose, in short, that we draw the line *in the middle*.

It is worth noting that this is close to what is happening

anyway, constrained both by biological facts (more than 90 percent of all abortions occur in the first trimester) and by evolving policy. The 1973 Supreme Court decision in *Roe v. Wade* allows states to regulate abortions more stringently as the fetus matures, and many states have done so. Later Court decisions allow states to impose certain restrictions, such as waiting periods, though not others, such as parental notification. What we have been doing, in effect, is carving out a compromise, an integrative middle position. It is left to us now to insist that this position is not somehow disgraceful or weak-willed or politically second-best, but instead a clear-headed (and long overdue) acknowledgment of the diversity of values at stake and an attempt to answer at least partly to both (all) of them.

Chapter 3 suggested that a still more constructive approach would address the demand for abortion itself. Remember the Wisconsin legislation described in that chapter, for example. Both sides supported it. We could go much further along these lines. Early in 1994 a group was formed called the Common Ground Network for Life and Choice: a coalition of activists from both sides—life and choice—seeking to move beyond the current deadlock, listening to each other, for once, rather than rehearsing the old attacks. It's a good sign. Possibly, as chapter 3 suggests, more truly integrative solutions are finally on the horizon.

One last reflection. Maybe the temptation to polarize values is already present in the very term "conflicts of values." Merely to speak of "conflict" makes it seem that there is not much to be done, as in the headlines that come so quickly to mind, like "The Abortion Issue: A Conflict of Rights." It sounds as if we must just choose. Even our language, then, might be rethought. Suppose that instead of calling such cases "conflicts of values," we just take them as reminders that our values are complicated, that usually many concerns must be addressed at once. Just that. Such issues are not necessarily head-on collisions of different values where one and only one side must finally win. They may instead be opportunities for the creative integration of values. Let us try to use them better.

Notes and Comments

On the necessary complexity of ethical issues, see my book *Toward Better Problems* (Philadelphia: Temple University Press, 1992), chapter 2. For a rich and compelling defense of pluralism in our ethical life, see Michael Walzer, *Spheres of Justice* (New York: Basic Books, 1983). Christopher Stone's *Earth and Other Ethics* (New York: Harper & Row, 1987) is another defense of pluralism—especially the necessity of integrative strategies—in ethics. Likewise, philosopher Martin Benjamin has written a useful book on compromise in ethics: *Splitting the Difference* (Lawrence: University Press of Kansas, 1990). Given the plurality of values, Benjamin argues, what he calls "integrity-preserving compromise" is not only possible but sometimes even required in ethics.

On abortion in particular, see *Toward Better Problems*, pp. 39–53. A revealing social and historical study of the abortion debate is Kristin Luker, *Abortion and the Politics of Motherhood* (Berkeley: University of California Press, 1984).

The quote from Dewey is from his essay "The Construction of Good," chapter 10 of his book *The Quest for Certainty*, reprinted in James Gouinlock, *The Moral Writings of John Dewey* (New York: Hafner-Macmillan, 1976), p. 154. The general theme of integrating values is thoroughly Deweyan, as Gouinlock's collection makes clear.

The quotation from Stephen Covey is from his book *The Seven Habits of Highly Effective People* (New York: Simon & Schuster, 1989), p. 273.

There is an interesting social-psychological literature on integrative strategies, some of which suggests that competitive, polarized struggles can be defused simply by reconceptualizing the issues at hand as problems that are solvable in a cooperative, mutually acceptable way. The results are demonstrably better for everyone, even by purely self-interested standards. See Dean Pruitt and Steven Lewis, "The Psychology of Integrative Bargaining," in Daniel Druckman, ed., *Negotiation: A Social-Psychological Perspective* (London: Sage, 1977).

Time's "Owl versus Man" cover appeared on June 25, 1990. For background on the integrative approach to "Owls versus Man" suggested in the text, see the accompanying article (which, interestingly, is not at all as polarized as the cover suggests) and John B. Judis, "Ancient Forests, Lost Jobs," *In These Times* 14:31 (August 1-14, 1990). A thorough study concluding that environmentalism and economic welfare are not at odds—that in fact they go together—is Stephen Meyer, *Environmentalism and Economic Prosperity* (Cambridge, MA: MIT Project on Environmental Politics and Policy, 1992).

As I say in the text, I don't mean to imply that relatively happy, integrative solutions are always possible. Nothing guarantees that all good things are compatible. Indeed, given the many sources of our values, it is almost guaranteed that they are not. Some choices are tragic. Others are at least hard.

Still, these undeniable facts do not justify the short shrift that integrative methods tend to get in ethics. Sometimes it may be true, in the face of conflicting values, that the best we can do is to choose one side. Even here, though, we should not conceive our task as picking a "right" way over a "wrong" one. We must try instead to choose the *greater* good. A *better* way, not the "right" one. In the "Owl versus Man" case, for instance, even if we really do have to pick a side, we should ask not which side is right but which side is better. Environmentalists may argue, for example, that while preserving jobs is certainly important, the very survival of the owls is at stake: it's life or death for the owls but not for the loggers. Also, the old-growth forests are almost all gone already, so some change for loggers is inevitable. Put this way, the environmentalist argument does not polarize values. It is only a comparison. A few more years of relative stability for loggers is important, but not as important as the probable destruction of a species forever and of a precious ecosystem for a very long time.

It may seem that this way of thinking relocates conflicts but does nothing to resolve them. After all, how do we tell which is the greater good? I think, however, that it is a radical improvement to weigh the merits of the conflicting positions rather than reject all but one as wrong. Moreover—and this is the main point—the natural next step is to seek an alternative that incorporates the best of both conflicting positions: that is, to look for compromises or creative ways of going beyond compromise. Polarizing values, by contrast, leads only to further entrenchment and conflict.

Instructors may wish to use the integrative turn suggested in this chapter as an entry point for discussing and/or surveying ethical theories. Let me conclude this section by outlining and then commenting on the theoretical strategy.

The great attraction of ethical theory, viewed in this context, is its integrative character. The aim is not merely to harmonize values but to actually unify them under a single heading. Conflicting values end up playing their partial roles in a single, inclusive network of considerations all derived, in the end, from a few (or, ideally, one) basic principles. Apparent conflicts on one level can then be resolved (in "principle", anyway) by referring to the more basic principles from which the conflicting values themselves supposedly arise. Looked at this way, the theoretical strategy is—or hopes to be—maximally integrative.

For example, one common kind of theory takes *happiness* (pleasure, satisfaction, welfare, positive states of mind) as its main concern and focuses on increasing or maximizing happiness, both by producing more positive states of mind and reducing negative states of mind, e.g., suffering. Its basic principle is the familiar "Seek the greatest good for the greatest number," where "good" means happiness. This kind of theory is called "utilitarian."

Approaching an issue like "Owl versus Man," for instance, utilitarians try to calculate how much happiness and suffering are at stake on each side. Utilitarians would advise us to weigh our positive experiences of owls and forests (or simply of knowing that they are there) against the negative experiences threatened by the loss of some loggers' livelihoods and corporate profits. This is not necessarily easy, but it is not impossible either: it is a method widely used in public policymaking, though still controversial. Its great advantage, according to the ethical theorist, is that at least we have some kind of common measure, some unity to values as a basic point of reference.

Another kind of theory takes *respect* as its main concern. People (and possibly other creatures and/or some institutions) are said to have basic dignity and worth, to which it is our obligation to respond with respect. Often this is described in the language of rights: we are said to have rights, such as life, liberty, and the pursuit of happiness, on which others may not infringe. This kind of theory is often called "deontological."

Approaching an issue like abortion, for instance, deontologists might consider the basis of the different rights in conflict. Does the fetus have a right to life, for instance, and if so, on what basis? Some argue that the fetus has a right to life in the name of its future personhood. Others argue that it does not, on the grounds that in every other case we attribute rights only on the basis of *present* capacities and interests. There are complicated and subtle arguments on both sides.

The classic statement of utilitarianism is John Stuart Mill's *Utilitarianism,* which is available in many editions. The classic statement of deontology is Immanuel Kant, *Foundations of the Metaphysics of Morals,* also available in many editions (sometimes under the title *Grounding for the Metaphysics of Morals*). A quite different and experience-based approach to respect for others is Martin Buber, *I and Thou* (translated by Walter Kaufmann and published by Scribner's). There are also many other theories and types of theories. Most introductory ethics textbooks offer a representative survey.

Theoretical unity is appealing intellectually and also practically. It may help solve some conflicts. Thinking of the abortion issue in terms of rights, for example, may help us clarify which considerations are most compelling. Theories of rights usually imply rankings of rights or perhaps set standards for having rights that not all parties to a conflict of values may meet. Though there is still room for argument about how to apply such rankings or standards, at least there is a definite framework within which to proceed.

Theories may also lead us to new ethical positions by drawing out the parallels between ethical judgments that we already accept and others that the theory suggests we should accept. This is a common strategy in animal rights arguments, for example. The arguments proceed by suggesting that some animals are not very different from humans in regard to what it takes to have rights. Apes should have rights, they say, if human children do.

Then too, a theory may compel by its sheer beauty. Surely it is not a small thing to figure out how all of our values hang together. Behind the apparent multiplicity and chaos there may be a strict and striking kind of order. To find such an order can be a revelation.

We should conclude, though, on a note of caution. Though theories at their best may be highly integrative, theory in practice readily tends in the opposite direction. People appeal to theories to justify their favorite values and rule the competing values out of court entirely. In this case, polarized values on the practical level are only restated, in a more formal, abstract, and thus more entrenched and resistant way, on the theoretical level. For a sobering account of this process at work in medical ethics, see Richard Zaner, *Ethics and the Clinical Encounter* (Englewood Cliffs, NJ: Prentice-Hall, 1988), chapter 1.

The turn to ethical theory is rarely defended as such. Perhaps this is because, for many philosophers, philosophy itself is virtually identical to the theoretical project, so the idea of defending the theoretical move in philosophy hardly comes up. Besides, probably the best defense of the theoretical project as such is simply a good theory ("see, it can be done!"), so most of the effort continues to go into the development and defense of (what we hope are) better theories. Still, critics of the turn to theory have a variety of complaints. Albert Jonsen and Stephen Toulmin have shown that there are other ways to systematize values, and argue about them rationally, besides the theoretical, top-down way (*The Abuse of Casuistry* [Berkeley: University of California Press, 1988]). Bernard Williams has argued that there is no reason to suppose that the "truth" about ethics, if there is such a thing at all, is simple in the way that a theory could capture: see his aptly named *Ethics and the Limits of Philosophy* (Cambridge, MA: Harvard University Press, 1985). Chapter 4 of Benjamin's book is good on this point as well. Feminist writers have argued that theoretical ethics causes us to lose sight of the richness and diversity of real values: see the essays in Eva F. Kittay and Diana Meyers, *Women and Moral Theory* (Totowa, NJ: Rowman and Littlefield, 1986), and Margaret Walker, "Moral Understandings," Hypatia 4 (1989), pp. 15–28. My book *Toward Better Problems* warns that the theoretical approach also tends to block nontheoretical modes of engagement or problem-solving.

From a practical point of view, I think that the best approach to ethical theories is itself integrative. That is, when faced with conflicting theories, just as when faced with conflicting values, we ought to ask not which one is right, but what each one is right *about*. Each may help illuminate certain aspects of a problematic situation, including aspects that would otherwise be overlooked. Each may offer an especially powerful way to articulate some of the values at stake. Let us call on them for these things. If the screws begin to tighten, however, and we are told that we can only think about ethical values in terms of one or another theory, it is time to pay more attention to the other values that are probably being pushed off the stage. There are no reasons to force unity, and as I have been at pains to argue, effective and creative problem-solving in no way depends upon it.

5

Ethics with a Heart

—ɯ—

Ethics asks us to resist closed-heartedness, to keep the heart open. This too is a kind of mindfulness—perhaps it is the most fundamental kind of all—and it is the last of our major themes in practical ethics.

WHEN THE HEART CLOSES

You are being served at a restaurant—or bank, ticket window, checkout counter, or a dozen other such places. Everyone knows how automatic and taken-for-granted such a relationship can be. Indeed it is seldom a "relationship" at all. For customers, all too often, waiters are just a way of getting food. For waiters, a customer may be just another mouth. This can be true even if there is some dialogue or maybe even flirtation going on. Everyone may just be playing a role, with hardly a second thought—with hardly a thought for the person on the other side.

What is happening here? In cases like these, we seem to be unable to project ourselves into others' situations, unwilling to imagine their feelings as if they were ours. The nineteenth-century philosopher Josiah Royce describes it almost biblically:

> Thou hast regarded [thy neighbor's] thought, his feeling, as somehow different from thine. Thou hast said, "A pain in him is not like a pain in me, but something far easier to bear." He seems to thee a little less living than thou. . . . So, dimly and by instinct hast thou lived with thy neighbor, and hast known him not, being blind. Thou hast made [of him] a thing, no Self at all.

This is what it means to have a closed heart. To put it in a more modern way, closed-heartedness is our tendency to forget that the people around us have the same kinds of feelings and needs as we do. It is our tendency to treat others like things, like servants or obstacles, rather than truly like other people.

Oh, someone will say, that's too extreme. We certainly do know, all of the time or most of the time, that others are people too.

But consider: we hardly even notice when human bank tellers are replaced with automatic teller machines. Why? Possibly because we were treating the tellers like machines all along? This is what Royce means when he says that we live with each other "dimly and by instinct." We treat others as if they had "no Self at all." So often we relate to each other out of pure habit, automatically.

Royce is even literally right when he says that we discount other people's pain. Think of what happens when doctors suddenly become patients: when surgeons go under the knife or anesthesiologists get anesthesia. A common reaction is shock. The injection that for years they told patients "just hurts a little" turns out to hurt like hell. Procedures that are routine to them suddenly become frightening and new. The attitudes of other doctors—their own attitudes, too, up to that moment—begin to seem strange and hard-hearted.

Why didn't they see it before? After all, they're only experiencing the same thing they've seen for years from a different point of view. But sometimes it seems that point of view is everything. As the old joke goes, when some doctors say "it won't hurt at all," what they really mean is that it won't hurt *them*. (Royce again: "Thou hast said, 'A pain in him is not like a pain in me, but something far easier to bear'"). For some doctors, patients' pain is something to be "managed," not something to be shared and sympathized with.

We easily recognize and resent this kind of closed-heartedness when we're on the receiving end. Nothing is so chilling as knowing that you are only a thing to someone else. Cheery salespeople greet me on the phone like an old friend but hang up in mid-sentence when they realize that they are not going to make a sale. And it gets much worse. Sexual exploitation—realizing that you are only a body to someone else, only a means to someone else's momentary pleasure— is far more deeply chilling. All trust, all sense of standing as one person among others, is betrayed. We complain, as Royce did, that "you're just treating me like an object" or "like a thing, not a person."

Cases in which people are completely reduced to things are among the greatest of evils. The Nazi concentration camps were meant to dehumanize: it is no surprise that they were the first step toward mass slaughter. Slavery meant the literal treatment of human beings as no more than property and was partly rationalized by the claim that blacks did not really feel physical pain or suffer under oppression in the way whites would. (Once again: "A pain in him is not like a pain in me.") It has been said many times, of many people and peoples. Scientists said it, and some still say it, of other animals. Closed-heartedness is tempting—and all too common.

Why the Heart Closes

To resist closing our hearts, we must understand why it happens. Here are some of the ways.

The primary villain, according to many moral philosophers, is self-centeredness. We don't see or hear others because our own selves loom so large. Sometimes we simply ignore others, are oblivious to them, so full are we of our selves. This is why some people can live for years in a family or other group and yet never have a clue about what anyone else is feeling. What *I'm* feeling is just too important.

Self-centeredness also leads us to read into others what we want to see there. A man wants the object of his desire to feel the same toward him; therefore, he concludes that she does, and acts accordingly. He is not interested in—and in fact may be a little afraid of—finding out what she really thinks.

So self-centeredness is part of the story. But there are other factors too. For one, there is simple practical need. Life is too complicated and too demanding to always relate in a completely connected way. We do need to get our food at the restaurant and our money at the bank, and maybe even to sell each other things over the phone. Sometimes we probably do have to live with each other "dimly and by instinct," relating to other people, even our closest family and friends, a little automatically, a little "blindly." Sometimes. The problem arises when we relate to other people *only* in this automatic way. Habit can take over. When we relate to more and more people mostly as if they were automatic teller machines or patients to be managed, then we may lose the ability to relate in any other way.

Disparaging language and stereotypes also play a variety of roles in closing our hearts. Sometimes our language literally reduces a person, or a whole group of people, to things. When men refer to women by their sexual parts, for example, they treat women as sex objects—that is, as objects, bodies, to be used for sexual purposes. Other common male words for women, like "chick," "babe," or "doll," name mindless or helpless playthings or dependents. These terms teach both men and women to see women that way.

Stereotypes call forth routine and immediate responses, again keeping us from relating to other people as people and substituting automatic reactions. Imagine encountering someone completely new, about whom you have no preconceptions or expectations. If you have no labels to apply to this person, you actually need to *relate*. But this is very different from what usually happens. Usually we come well equipped with labels. All we need to know is that someone is a Republican, or homeless, or a lawyer, or even just a stranger, and we know "who they are." Appearance alone is often enough to bring out our stereotypes. No need to relate; just react.

Stereotypes also create or exaggerate differences that serve to keep our hearts closed. Someone who is different from you seems less important too, and perhaps even, as Royce puts it, "a little less living" as well. So (some) whites define themselves as different from blacks, (some) men define themselves as different from women, Christians as different from Jews, Americans as different from non-Americans, and all of us as different from animals. The real differences may in fact be irrelevant or may not even exist, but it hardly matters. The alleged differences keep us from paying attention, and once we stop paying attention, we're not likely to notice that the stereotypical differences are only imaginary.

Self-fulfilling Prophecies

Worse, stereotypes like these can become self-fulfilling. For example, one of the chief excuses for the enslavement of blacks in America was that black people were naturally "ignorant and depraved." But one of the prime effects of slavery was that the slaves were often *made* ignorant and depraved. They were kept unschooled, stultified with work, their families and communities broken again and again. Thus, as the anti-slavery campaigner Frederick Douglass pointed out, "the very crimes of slavery become slavery's best defense. By making the enslaved a character fit only for slavery, they excuse themselves for failing to make the slave a freeman." Slavery wears down and degrades the slave; then this very degradation is blamed on the slaves themselves, thus justifying more slavery and still more degradation.

Much the same can be said, in a milder way perhaps, about the effects of other kinds of prejudice. Sexism, for example, can also become a self-fulfilling prophecy. All manner of prejudicial barriers wear down and consume a woman, and then her own failures are held up as proof that sexism is justified.

There are also examples beyond the sphere of human relations. Think of animals in factory farms: treated like living egg or milk machines or living pieces of meat, unable in many cases even to turn around or to do anything natural.

Soon they genuinely become unsociable, incapable, and pitiful—not to mention dangerous to themselves and others. People who know such animals are often genuinely puzzled about how anyone could think that they have rights or moral standing—the animals seem so pitiful. But the fact that the animals are reduced to such a state is precisely the objection. They are *made* pitiful. Our own hard hearts first allow and then perhaps contribute to the animals' degradation, and then that very degradation seems to justify still harder hearts.

HOW THE HEART OPENS

I began this chapter with Royce's indictment of our closed-heartedness. Now Royce goes on:

> Have done with this illusion, and simply try to learn the truth. Pain is pain, joy is joy, everywhere, even as in thee. . . . In all exultation and hope, everywhere, from the noblest to the lowest, the same conscious, burning, willful life is found, endlessly manifold as the forms of the living creatures, unquenchable as the fires of the sun, real as these impulses that even now throb in thine own heart.

Remaining open to this fact I will call "open-heartedness." To put it in a more modern way, open-heartedness is our ability to remember that the people around us have the same feelings and needs as we do. It is to know, and not just say, that other people are people too.

Recognizing when and why we often close our hearts is a start toward opening them. We can acknowledge our own self-centeredness but then put it in its place. We can take more care with our language. We can take our stereotypes with more than a few grains of salt. We can try to break some of our habitual and automatic ways of relating to other people. Treat the waitress like a person (how would you feel if you were in her shoes?) rather than like a food-toting robot or someone whose sole purpose in life is to meet your needs.

With the question "How would you feel if you were in her shoes?" we come back to the Golden Rule. I said in Chapter 2 that the Golden Rule is not really a rule at all in the sense that it gives us a way to make specific decisions. But it has other uses. To say "Do unto others as you would have them do unto you" is essentially to say: remember that others are just as real, just as conscious, just as important as you. And that is a crucial reminder. It is one important way past our self-centeredness.

The requirement is not that we treat other people in exactly the way we treat ourselves. It is that we treat other people as something more and different than simply things: at least that we treat other people with some degree of courtesy and acknowledgment. Recognizing that other people have some kind of inner life, as we do, and figuring out what it is—moving past the stereotypes, past the labels, past our own prejudices and a world that often reproduces and reinforces them.

One of my students wrote about meeting a homeless woman in New York's Penn Station.

> I was waiting for a friend, but she was late and I was all alone and scared. A woman who was selling spin tops outside the station saw me and came over to me. She asked my name and I told her and she said her name was Mona Lisa. We ended up talking for an hour and a half. . . . She told me all about her life and how she ended up in the streets of New York. All for love. Her boyfriend was black and she was white and her parents were going to disown her so she ran away with him and they are still together, in love. . . .

A country kid, alone and frightened on a first visit to New York, approached by a kind of person she had never known face to face, who she knew only as a stereotype—*the Homeless*—repeated a thousand times on television and in the newspapers. Still, this student found herself able to see her and respond to her as a person, as "Mona Lisa" did in return.

Notice that responding in this way is not the same as just being "nice." To be nice would have been to buy a spin top and back away: to stay on the level of habit and stereotyped response. This student did something entirely different. She responded as one person to another. ("She did not treat me as a customer to buy a spin top but as a scared friend. And I did not treat her as a bag lady but a confidant.") Something much more valuable than money or spin tops was exchanged that night.

Minding the Golden Rule, then, is one route to open-heartedness. Here are some other suggestions.

Be prepared for surprises. One way to a closed heart, remember, is sheer habit: our tendency to relate to others automatically and out of stereotype and routine. To open our hearts, we need to take the opposite tack. Break the routine. For example, deliberately look for what goes against the stereotypes. Remind yourself that you do not know every-thing there is to know about a person just on the basis of his or her appearance or a few labels. I have learned more from my mentally retarded brother than from many of my teach-ers. But to most people he is just "retarded." They can't see past the labels. Likewise, no one is just a "chick" or a lawyer or a fundamentalist—any more than *you* could be reduced to such a label. Be prepared to notice.

Learn to keep still sometimes. One of the chief obstacles to really seeing or hearing other people is all the interfer-ence coming from ourselves. Train yourself to turn it off for a while. You can always turn it back on later (if you want to). But when you are listening, listen wholeheartedly. Don't judge—just listen.

Reach out to others. Give people a chance. Remember how easily patterns of closed-heartedness can become self-fulfilling. Then consider the parallel point, that patterns of open-heartedness can become self-fulfilling too. So say hello to people on the street, and see what kind of goodwill comes back to you. Offer a troubled child or a troubled friend some love or trust, rather than just moralizing in the hope that maybe someday they will deserve it. *You* take the first step. Trust first—invite them to live up to it.

In a burst of inspiration, someone once set up a program at an urban senior center that brings in ex-convicts, their last shot at rehabiliation, to help the elderly. "Because maybe this center's a last shot for some of these old folks too. Last shot for companionship, last shot before dying, alone. Both groups on the edge—why not bring them together?" So an ex-con and an old woman walk down the street together. She was once mugged by someone like him. Now he helps with the shopping. She says:

> I don't know what he sees in me. All I know, he walks me home. We talk and joke. I learn things about how things are in the world now, which I don't know much about anymore. And I don't get the feeling that I'm just a little old Jewish lady. You think that's nothing? You know how many other people I don't feel like a little old lady with?

He says:

> Try to shake having been a junkie and done time, man. Everywhere you go, you get that. But this woman, it's like she doesn't care. She says she had a hard life too, maybe that's it. I told her how I robbed things. I told her about jail. She says,

"Your mother must have been very upset. Let's get groceries. You have time to do that?" Nobody ever treated me like I had anything to give. Just to take. So that's all I ever did. Take. . . .

"It's a chance to break out of the old patterns," says the founder of the program. No kidding. Chances were taken all around. Give people a chance—take a chance yourself.

THE EXPANDING CIRCLE

Because ethics calls for open-heartedness, ethics is also open-*ended*. The circle of our ethical concern tends to grow: to become more and more inclusive.

Slavery, for one obvious example, was common in the ancient world. It was taken for granted. No moral questions were raised. It was also widespread in the not so distant past in Europe and America. Now we recognize it for the evil it was. More recently, the civil rights movement brought racism into focus as a moral evil, although this fight is far from over. Now we are beginning to recognize sexism—discrimination against women—as similarly widespread and similarly unacceptable, though here too the fight is only beginning.

Change in such cases is a lot more difficult than it seems after the fact. From slave-owners' point of view, it was unimaginable that slaves could somehow be their equals and deserve the same human respect. Slavery was just the way things were. It was taken for granted. It was embraced and practiced by all the right people. The science and religion of the day both rationalized it. Besides, as Frederick Douglass pointed out, slavery sometimes degraded the slaves so far that their enslavement seemed to be justified. They did not seem like equals. That slavery might be called into question was almost unimaginable—until it was.

How did the question even arise? As with any major social change, there were a variety of causes. For one thing, not everyone in slave societies had a stake in slavery. In the United States in the mid-19th century, major economic interests had begun to push the other way. Also, at least a few voices within the dominant moral and religious traditions had always spoken out against slavery. There were periodic slave revolts too, though they were violently put down.

Beneath and beyond these forces, a basic moral process was also at work. Some people—perhaps at first only a few—were willing and able to identify with the enslaved race: to put themselves into the position of a slave, to see the slaves as people like themselves, suffering as they would. They began to question the "obvious" idea that race could make such an enormous moral difference that one race could be free and another enslaved. Gradually they found a voice and went to work on the hearts and minds of others. The old excuses began to ring hollow.

Great forces are in tension at moments like this. On the one side, the old habits and norms remain powerful. No one wants to think that a whole way of life, comfortable and normal to most people, may still prove morally unacceptable, and may have to change. Yet our hearts can pull us in another direction. It may become more and more apparent that the old ways have to change.

Philosopher Tom Regan wonders what he would have done in the days when the religious and scientific rationalizations for slavery were still widely accepted:

> I play this question over and over again in my imagination. I know what I want to believe. I want to believe that I would have been one among those who agitated for change in the moral status quo—one among the minority who saw through the flimsy fabric of prejudice, ignorance, and fear that barred

acceptance of all humans as morally equal, each to all. But. . .
I do not know. The power of the dominant culture . . . is
great. . . .

There is no reliable guide in such situations. But we can
at least recognize that sometimes the moral status quo may
be wrong—and recognize that sometimes it is the heart that
tells us first. Be ready to listen.

Is any moral status quo in question today? Regan thinks
so. Consider, he says, our treatment of other animals.

We are used to thinking of animals as lesser creatures,
indeed hardly as creatures at all: as mere resources available
to serve our needs. Commercially raised chickens spend
their whole short lives in cages too small to allow them to
turn around. Veal calves are deprived of nutrients, exercise,
and even light. Large numbers of dogs, chimps, cats, rabbits,
and many other animals are used each year to test new drugs
and chemicals for eventual human use.

Yet the plight of these animals has begun to speak to us.
Here too, some people have been willing and able to listen:
to put themselves in the position of other creatures, to see
other animals as beings like ourselves, suffering as we
would. They are beginning to question the "obvious" idea
that species makes such an enormous moral difference that
beings of one species are morally special while those of all
other species can be mercilessly exploited. Perhaps they are
wrong—perhaps other animals really do not deserve full-
fledged moral consideration—but their voices are certainly
becoming harder to rationalize away.

All the old dismissals of animals are still with us. Animals
can't think, people say; they don't feel pain, and on and on.
For most people, eating animals is still so normal as to seem
unquestionable. Many of my students literally believe that
they cannot live without it. But people are changing too. Veg-

etarianism is on the rise, and most restaurants now serve non-meat dishes. The old habits may no longer be good enough. Even people who continue to eat meat are beginning to feel obliged to make excuses for it, which is at least a sign that they feel some tension. Moral unease is growing. Perhaps in a hundred years we will find the current treatment of animals unbelievable, much as we now find slavery unbelievable. Or perhaps we won't. In any case, the question is now open.

Ethics is also trying to respond to the environmental crisis. Some philosophers and moralists are arguing that we must begin to view all of nature ethically. Perhaps we must now take a new look not merely at other animals but at whole ecosystems, even at the whole living Earth. The circle may grow very wide indeed.

Here crisis pushes us, to be sure, but once again there is a pull too. We are beginning to recognize the enormous creativity, complexity, and depth of the rest of the world: the nonhuman, the other-than-human, the more-than-human. The grandeur and magic of nature, the silence-that-is-not-stillness of the wild, the glittering stars, birds everywhere, the very continents gliding about on molten oceans of rock; and on and on. It has been easy to overlook all of this, to ignore it, to turn a blind eye to it even when it is right next to us: and therefore we also easily destroy it. Human exploitation of nature has been with us a long time. It too is a habit, a comfortable, normal way of life. Yet it too is now perhaps becoming questionable. Twenty years ago, we could not have imagined even something now as basic as recycling bins in everyone's basement or whale songs on CD. Who knows what another twenty years will bring? A new period of umimagined ethical growth may be upon us.

So ethics is not a closed book. Our values, and our ways of living them out, have changed many times and will change again. The circle is expanding, and our sympathies and our understanding behind its leading edge are expanding and deepening too. This is part of what makes ethics so difficult—and so exciting. Stay with it. And keep both an open heart and an open mind.

Notes and Comments

The quotes from Josiah Royce can be found in *The Religious Aspect of Philosophy* (Boston: Houghton Mifflin, 1885), pp. 157–162. For further reading along these lines, more difficult but also more suggestive, try Martin Buber, *I and Thou*, trans. Walter Kaufmann (New York: Scribner, 1970).

On sexual language as stereotyping, see Robert Baker, "'Chicks' and 'Pricks': A Plea for Persons," in Robert Baker and Frederick Elliston, eds. *Philosophy and Sex* (Buffalo, NY: Prometheus Books, 1975). The citation from Frederick Douglass on p. 72 is from his speech "The Claims of the Negro Ethnologically Considered" in *The Frederick Douglass Papers*, Series One, vol. 2 (New Haven, CT: Yale University Press, 1982), p. 507. For more on self-fulfilling prophecies in ethics, see my paper "Self-Validating Reduction: Toward a Theory of the Devaluation of Nature", *Environmental Ethics* 18 (1996) 115–132, and my book *Back to Earth: Tomorrow's Environmentalism* (Philadelphia: Temple University Press, 1994), pp. 94–105.

On prejudice in general, see Gordon Allport's classic *The Nature of Prejudice* (Reading, MA: Addison-Wesley, 1954). Jean-Paul Sartre, in *Anti-Semite and Jew* (New York: Schocken, 1948), analyzes the peculiar psychology of prejudice against Jews in a way that has a striking and wide resonance.

The account of meeting a homeless woman in Penn Station was an anonymous answer to a short writing assignment in one of my ethics classes on Buber's *I and Thou*. For one striking account, along much the same lines, of a former Klansman's evolution out of racism, read the interview with C. P. Ellis in Studs Terkel's book *American Dreams: Lost and Found* (New York: Ballantine, 1980), pp. 221–233. The account of the ex-cons at the senior center is one of many stories in Ram Dass and Paul Gorman's wonderful book *How Can I Help? Stories and Reflections on Service* (New York: Knopf, 1985).

A variety of approaches are possible to the question of self-centeredness. Some ethical philosophers define ethics in such a way that it is opposed to egoism by definition. In *Foundations of the Metaphysics of Morals*, Kant argued that ethics requires impartiality as opposed to our usual "partiality" to ourselves. David Hume, by contrast, argued that egoism is a radically incomplete picture of human nature, and thus is readily overcome simply by appeals to fellow-feeling and sympathy. See his *Enquiry Concerning the Principles of Morals*, Section V and Appendix II. I agree with Hume, and in this chapter I am concerned primarily with the psychological and social factors that tend to block what Hume would call the generalization of our sympathies. However, this approach is not exactly incompatible with the Kantian view. Kant would push it outside of ethics proper, but it remains no less compelling a practical question.

Another, rather different response to the problem of egoism is the "No-Self" philosophy of certain kinds of Eastern thought, notably Zen Buddhism. See Shunryu Suzuki, *Zen Mind, Beginner's Mind* (New York: Weatherhill, 1970). A nice application of Zen thinking to the real-life situation of college students is Inge Bell, *This Book Is Not Required* (Fort Bragg, CA: The Small Press, 1991).

The image of an expanding ethical circle was used by Peter Singer in a book by the same title: *The Expanding Circle* (New York: Farrar, Straus, and Giroux, 1981), pp. 111-124. Singer's book *Animal Liberation* (New York: Avon, 1991), and Tom Regan's *The Case for Animal Rights* (Berkeley: University of California Press, 1983), are the classic philosophical defenses of the ethical status of other animals. Regan proceeds from rights theory, Singer from utilitarianism. For a richly textured and less theoretical ethical approach to other animals, see Mary Midgley's work, for example *Animals and Why They Matter* (Athens, GA: University of Georgia Press, 1983).

The citation from Regan on p. 78 is from an unpublished paper titled "Patterns of Resistance: The Struggle for Freedom and Equality in America," quoted by permission.

On the extension of ethics to the whole ecosphere, the classic source is Aldo Leopold, *A Sand County Almanac* (New York: Oxford University Press, 1949). The opening of the last essay in that book, "The Land Ethic," also draws upon the image of an expanding circle. There are a number of good contemporary anthologies on environmental ethics, such as Christine Pierce and Donald Vandeveer, eds., *People, Penguins, and Plastic Trees* (Belmont, CA: Wadsworth, 1986, 1995), and Susan Armstrong and Richard Botzler, eds., *Environmental Ethics* (New York: McGraw-Hill, 1993). My book *Back to Earth*, cited above, represents a experience-based approach to expanding circles.

A Word to Students
How to Write an Ethics Paper

—∿—

This book presents ethics primarily as a mode of action, and accordingly we have been concerned mainly with practical skills. In academic contexts, however, ethics is usually taught as a subject, and one of the primary skills called into play is writing. This appendix therefore offers some guidelines for writing an ethics paper.

GETTING STARTED

The first rule in writing any academic paper is: understand the assignment. You need to understand what kind of audience you should address and what topic or range of topics should be covered.

You will almost always write more clearly and consistently if you keep in mind a vivid picture of the audience for whom you are writing. Besides, it is much easier to imagine yourself talking to your roommate or maybe even your senator than addressing an abstract void. So pick someone to write to. It may even be a person who will actually read your paper.

In one sense, obviously, you are writing for your teacher or professor. But he or she is usually not the best audience to keep in mind as you write. What you may need to say in your paper is not necessarily what you would say to your teacher in direct conversation. For example, teachers generally expect that student papers will competently review the subject matter, but the subject will seldom be news to the teacher. You need to imagine writing for someone who could really use the explanation. I tell my students to imagine writing for a friend or roommate who is not in the class but who is, like them, intelligent and interested.

If the appropriate audience is not clear, ask.

A specific topic may be assigned by your teacher, or the choice of topic may be left to you. If the choice is left to you, pick something that interests you and allows you to say something constructive. After all, ethics is about real life; choose a real topic. Once again, if you are not sure whether a certain topic is appropriate, ask.

Once you know your audience, your next step is to choose a voice. In other words, decide *how* to write the paper. Are you going to summarize the state of an argument in a professional voice? Are you going to tell a story that makes a point? Will there be a place for humor? For the personal? To express uncertainty?

Many professors expect abstract, impersonal writing as a matter of course. Many philosophers expect an argumentative style as well. Many, however, do not. Don't assume that these are your only options. For example, don't assume that

you must write in the same style as the articles and arguments you have been reading in class. Sometimes the point
of a writing assignment is to *react* to such readings. It may
be most effective and appropriate to react in a different
style.

Often you discover what and how you are going to write
only by actually writing. You do not need to decide for sure
before you even start. Just start. Imagine yourself speaking to
the person or audience you are addressing, and see what
happens. Of course, the virtue of doing this in your imagination (and, when writing, in very rough form) is that you can
start over—perhaps many times. Expect to write more than
one draft (this book, for example, has gone through about
twenty). You might try out several voices as you begin to
write and see which approach feels best. For more on writing and voice, see Part VI of Peter Elbow's *Writing with
Power* (New York: Oxford University Press, 1981). On the
matter of audience in particular, see Elbow's Chapter 20.

ARGUMENT PAPERS

In the remainder of this appendix, I outline two different
possible styles for ethics papers and offer specific guidelines
for each. I begin with the argument paper.

An argument paper in ethics is an attempt to define an
ethical position carefully and defend or criticize it using the
most general and plausible arguments you can find. It is a
paper whose aim is to prove a point.

Here are a few general guidelines for argument papers.

(1) Whether you are advancing your own argument or
criticizing someone else's, it is crucial to do so in an orderly
way. Don't jump right into criticism, or start by assuming the
ethical position that you want to try to establish. Start out
with a little background on the issue (remember your audi-

ence). Then it is helpful to summarize the argument you want to advance before developing it. Summarize it again when you are done.

If you are criticizing an argument, it is especially important to outline the argument first. Be sure to get it right. It is pointless to attack a position so extreme that no one holds it. Take time to explain the argument, explore in what ways it is plausible (there must be something plausible about it if people find it persuasive), and cite and perhaps quote some of its advocates. *Then* you are ready for criticism. Once again, it is helpful to summarize your criticism before you begin and again when you are done.

(2) Ethical arguments are partly factual arguments, so another necessary rule is: get your facts straight. Arguments about our treatment of other animals, for example, should include some relevant facts and statistics about how animals are treated. Arguments about assisted suicide should give a short history of this procedure and an up-to-date legal report. You may need to do some research.

Take care at this stage. Remember that, in ethics in particular, strong opinions may color the facts. Certainly they color presentations of the facts. So use a variety of sources, use reliable sources, carefully check the citations for any factual claims that are central to your argument or seem debatable (and cite the best sources in your own paper), and watch the reasoning, especially if the argument makes statistical claims or claims about causes. Arguments of this sort can be complex, uncertain, and tricky. An argument guide is useful here; see, for example, my *Rulebook for Arguments* (Indianapolis: Hackett, 1987, 1992).

(3) A somewhat less obvious but crucial rule is: clarify the principles upon which your argument is based.

Your ethics course will probably introduce and examine some common ethical principles, and illustrate the process of clarifying and reasoning about them. They may range from the fairly specific (like "Be honest on your taxes") to something quite general (like "Cause no unnecessary suffering") to the first principles of ethical theories (like "Seek the happiness of the greatest number").

Careful formulation of such principles is difficult. For example, fundamental legal issues often arise because it is unclear how previous legal principles apply to new situations. We have, for instance, a principle of parental rights. Legally, parents can decide where their underage children will live, what religion they follow (if any), or whether they go to public school or elsewhere (though not *whether* they are schooled), and so on. Still, there are areas of uncertainty. For example, can parents decide to deny their underage children lifesaving medical treatment? What about Jehovah's Witnesses, who can legally refuse blood transfusions for themselves on religious grounds? Can they also refuse blood transfusions for their underage children?

In cases like this, it is not enough to offer some vague generalization about "parental rights" as the relevant ethical or legal principle. The entire matter turns on exactly—and I mean *exactly*—what such principles say. Precisely how far do parental rights extend?

Your job, in addressing such a case, is to try to formulate a precise enough general principle to answer the specific question posed (such as "Should people with religious objections to blood transfusions be allowed refuse transfusions not only for themselves but also for their underage children?"). Your principle must plausibly answer the question. And it must not implausibly answer other practical questions that might be addressed to it.

For example, if you conclude that parents ought to be allowed to refuse such treatments because "parents have the right to make all fundamental religious choices for their underage children," then you may indeed have formulated a precise enough principle to answer the question. (You will need, though, to explain what you mean by "fundamental religious choices.") The principle may be plausible (argue for it). You might argue that the conclusion is plausible too. How, you might ask, could the law justifiably force blood into children's bodies against the religious beliefs that are followed by their parents and that the children themselves very likely accept or will accept as their own?

But this principle might have implausible implications as well. What if some children die as a result of being denied the blood? What if some parents' religion includes ritual torture or severe fasting? These are called "counterexamples": possible cases in which your proposed principle seems to leads to implausible consequences.

Your task in the face of such counterexamples is either to amend your proposed principle (and then consider whether its implications change in the original case, i.e., with respect to refusing transfusions) or to defend its apparently implausible implications: that is, to argue that the alleged counterexample doesn't refute the principle. (See my *Rulebook for Arguments*, section 11.) If you are criticizing someone else's argument, by contrast, arguing by counterexample may be exactly the strategy you want.

On the transfusion question, by the way, the law has tended in the opposite direction. Courts have taken custody of children in such cases and ordered transfusions. The relevant principle seems to be that the state has the right to protect children's lives until the children are old enough to decide for themselves. Note that this does not imply that the state has the right to force a decision on religiously unwilling parents when the matter does not involve life or death. (You might ask whether *this* principle has implausible practical implications too.)

Again, this is a difficult matter—more difficult than any short discussion such as this one can explain. If your teacher expects you to argue in this style in your paper, your assigned readings and classwork should offer you some practice and models to follow. For another model, or if no model is readily available, look at Peter Singer's article "Famine, Affluence, and Morality" in Christina and Fred Sommers, eds., *Vice and Virtue in Everyday Life*, third ed. (Fort Worth, TX: Harcourt, Brace, 1993). Singer's paper is a classic example of the argument style. He uses several widely agreeable moral principles and analogies to argue that we have an obligation to give some of our time and resources to help people who are starving (i.e., he argues that helping them is not just nice, but is *required*). You may or may not agree with him; I suggest his article here simply because his style is widely admired and emulated.

A response to Singer is John Arthur, "World Hunger and Moral Obligation," also in the Sommers and Sommers book. Another classic article, more difficult, is Judith Thompson's "A Defense of Abortion," also included in Sommers and Sommers and in a wide variety of other ethics anthologies. Thompson relies on several striking analogies to defend a woman's right to choose abortion even if the fetus also has a right to life—not an easy point to argue! Again, you may or may not agree; the point right now is to pay attention to her style.

DISCOVERY PAPERS

A discovery paper in ethics is an expression or exploration of an ethical position, usually linked to important events in the narrator's life or in our common experience. Often a discovery paper is a personal narrative or story, offered partly as a self-explanation and partly as an invitation for others to recognize something similar in their own experience.

Consider a famous essay by the novelist Alice Walker, "Am I Blue?", in her collection *Living by the Word* (San Diego: Harcourt Brace Jovanovich, 1988). It's very brief, only five pages or so, which describe her encounters with a horse named Blue and some of the thoughts and changes that resulted. Blue came to live in a field near her home. She fed him apples from a tree next to the field, where, she says, "I remained as thrilled as a child by his flexible dark lips, huge, cubelike teeth that crunched the apples, core and all, with such finality, and his high, broad-breasted enormity; beside which, I felt small indeed." But

> Blue was lonely. Blue was horribly lonely and bored. . . . Five acres to tramp by yourself, endlessly, even in the most beautiful of meadows. . . . cannot provide many interesting events, and once rainy season turned to dry that was about it. . . . I had forgotten that human animals and nonhuman animals can communicate quite well; if we are brought up around animals as children we take this for granted. It is in [animals'] nature to express themselves. What else are they going to express? And, generally speaking, they are ignored. (p. 5)

She begins to muse on the parallels to the treatment of black slaves, Native Americans, and sometimes the young: ignored too. The very possibility that they might have something of their own to communicate is often denied. Too often we see only our own reflections in those we subordinate and oppress.

She travels for a time. When she returns, Blue has a companion. "There was a new look in his eyes. A look of independence, of self-possession, of inalienable *horse*ness." There are weeks of a deep and mutual feeling of justice and peace. But eventually Blue's companion becomes pregnant: it turns out that she was "put with him" for that purpose. She is taken away.

Blue was like a crazed person. Blue *was*, to me, a crazed person. He galloped furiously . . . around and around his five acres. He whinnied until he couldn't. He tore the ground with his hooves . . . He looked always and always toward the road down which his partner had gone. And then, occasionally . . . , he looked at me. It was a look so piercing, so full of grief, a look so *human*, that I almost laughed (I felt too sad to cry) to think there are people who do not know animals suffer. (p. 7)

But they do. Again she is led to think about the suffering all around us and how too often we evade or deny that communication. The conclusion then is quick and stunning:

As we talked of freedom and justice one day for all, we sat down to steaks. I am eating misery, I thought, as I took the first bite. And spit it out. (p. 8)

Something happened here. Thinking about Blue helped Walker to draw connections between the experiences of human oppression that, as a black woman activist, she knew so well, and our exploitation of other animals. It was not merely abstract, either: Walker came to see her own actions in a different light, and the result was that at that moment she stopped eating meat.

Of course, as I just said about views like Singer's and Thompson's, you may not agree with the bottom line. In the same situation, you may have done something different. The point is that ethical discoveries do happen. You do not have to write as well as Walker either, of course, but you should try to capture the freshness and directness of your own experiences in the same way. A discovery paper is an exploration of when such things have happened *for you.*

* * *

Discovery papers in ethics use a much wider variety of styles than argument papers: people and their experiences are very different. Many approaches to writing are appropriate, from the simplest personal narratives to diary entries or poetry. Read enough of Natalie Goldberg's *Writing Down the Bones* (Boston: Shambhala Publications, 1986) to get some inspiration and some good advice.

Here are a few guidelines for discovery papers.

(1) Don't sentimentalize. You are writing about experience and what it meant to you, so you must speak the language of feeling, but this does not mean that everything must be described in terms of feeling or that the paper can simply emote. Notice that Walker is carefully descriptive even when she is speaking of highly emotional matters—for example, of Blue after his companion was taken away. Also, she is always drawing connections. The theme of animal communication, for example, runs throughout her essay, and it is this that makes the last lines so natural. So don't just tell us what you felt; tell us what happened, and what thoughts it provoked, and what you did about it, so that we may begin to think and feel and maybe even act the same way.

(2) Draw conclusions. Though the discovery style is much more personal than the argumentative style, remember that you are writing about the experience of values for a reason. You are not just reporting on yourself; you are opening up the question of ethical change and growth by so doing. You are suggesting, at least indirectly, that here are some questions that need ethical attention or here are some possibilities—new attitudes, new ways of life—that may call to us ethically.

For example, Walker is posing a specific question: how is it that we can so completely close our hearts to other creatures, and what might we do if our hearts were a little more open? Notice how beautifully her title opens that question. Am I Blue?, she asks. That is: in what ways is she herself, like Blue, a victim of oppression? The other side of the question is: how is she also like the oppressors? And what should she do about that? Part of her answer is to put down her fork.

In general, then, explore what you think are the larger implications of your experience. How did it change your sense of values? Why did it do this? How do these conclusions relate to the sense of values you brought to the experience? How do they relate to traditional values? And what did you or should you do about it? Your conclusions need not be extensive, but some attention to these questions is necessary.

Discovery papers are not argument papers (though you could combine the two styles—starting, for example, with a discovery and ending by trying to formulate principles). You do not need to draw conclusions that withstand test in a court of law. Instead your aim is to open up some new possibilities. Or to add a new dimension, or simply a new idea about values, to our already large stock of values, without implying that you have the last word or the whole story. Or to make some suggestions about how the circle of ethical concern is expanding, for you or for others, or deepening in ways we perhaps have not yet noticed. Discoveries are *beginnings*.

(3) Temper your conclusions with some reflections on the limits of your discovery or experience. Consider what it is about yourself (your background, your values, your lifestyle and dominant concerns) that may have made your discovery or experience possible.

Another way to ask this question is: how might you understand someone else who did not have the same experience you did? What factors may close off such experiences for some people or transform the experience into something else? Or again, are there other possible interpretations of the same experience? For example, Walker's reaction to the crisis in Blue's life was to stop eating meat. You might react quite differently—by trying to help Blue himself, for instance. Why do you think Walker changed in the way she did? Under what conditions might you or someone else change in a different way—or perhaps not change at all? If other people's experience is likely to be similar, what follows from that fact? If other people's experience is likely to be different, what follows from that fact?

There is much more to say about these things—more than any short discussion such as this one can cover. Again, though, if your teacher expects you to write in this style in your paper, your assigned readings should offer you some models to follow. Read the full version of Walker's "Am I Blue?". In fact, read the whole collection: Walker's essays are often models of intensely personal and critical ethical engagement in a discovery style. Another well-known essay you might examine is Philip Hallie's, "From Cruelty to Goodness," the first essay in the Sommers and Sommers collection. Hallie's is a scholar's story, the story of a search for (and discovery of) goodness in the midst of evil, in this case the Nazi holcaust. You might take it as a model of a discovery paper that goes beyond personal experience to a research project as well.

I should emphasize that the argument style and the discovery style hardly exhaust the options in ethics. They are only two common styles. Many others are also possible: dialogues, parables and sermons, stories, factual or journalistic accounts, "confessions," and so on. Your job in finding an ethical voice is partly to find (or create) the style or styles that work best for you.

Finally, whatever style you choose, I trust that as you plan and write your paper you will not forget all of the other advice offered in this book. Avoid mere appeals to authority. Try to think creatively about the options and alternatives in an ethically problematic situation. Integrate values rather than polarizing them. Keep an open heart and an open mind. Take your time—and give yourself the time to take.

A Word to Teachers
Some Suggestions
for Classroom Practice

—ɯ—

This final section offers some suggestions to instructors or group leaders about how to use this book in the classroom. I concentrate on the college ethics course, which is the course I teach and for which this book was primarily developed.

This book could be integrated into an ethics course in a variety of ways. In the most recent version of my own ethics course, I include the material in this book as part of the "ethical toolbox" with which the course opens. Also included are a quick survey of ethical theories (offered in an integrative spirit—that is, not as competitors for the "true" story about ethics, but as useful reminders about the many different dimensions of value often at stake when ethical problems arise) and some work on communicative and listening skills (offered not just as useful practical skills but also as a manifestation of an ethical attitude themselves—good listening, for example, is a manifestation of respect). In the rest of the course we put the tools to use as we consider a number of specific ethical issues chosen and developed by the class.

At other times, I use this book later in the term. Often I start my course with specific, direct, and intriguing moral challenges, like the question of love and friendship or of our relation to other animals. I like to assign some systematic and evocative works early on, such as Singer's *Animal Liberation* and Buber's *I and Thou*. The material in this book therefore fits better later, when our concerns turn more resolutely practical. So I may use only the opening chapters (1 and 2) as an introduction to the course, assigning the later chapters when we turn to practical problem-solving, and "A Word to Students" at paper-writing time. Chapter 5 is also a useful practical complement to theoretical readings in deontology.

Of course, there are other possibilities, too. This book is meant to be flexible. It is intended to be fairly self-sufficient as well: it need not require a lot of additional attention in courses that are already too full.

However you use this material, the real key is practice, practice, and practice. Also practice. Devise exercises for all of the skills you want to develop. Let me outline some of the exercises I use.

Chapter 1: This chapter argues that it is crucial to *think* about ethical matters—that feelings or personal opinions or dogmas are not enough. One of the underlying practical difficulties is that students often have no clear and attractive models of what ethical thinking can be like. Too often the models are talk-show scream-fests or manipulative political advertising. So you might arrange to offer some better models. Invite a friend or colleague to class and stage a conversation on some controversial topic in the reflective and considerate ways we want to promote. Invite students to join in the same key. Videotape it. Keep noting the contrasts to the usual ways of debating such issues. There are also some useful video resources, such as some of the debates in the WGBH/PBS series *The Constitution: That Delicate Balance*.

Another difficulty is that we often do not recognize when we are letting down our guard. Loaded language, for example, plays upon our emotional reactions, so that, as I say in the text, we are led into a prepackaged emotional commitment without ever thinking it through. A good countermeasure is to practice identifying loaded language in various statements, perhaps first in statements students disagree with and then in more congenial statements, including their own (have some class discussions on controversial topics, and videotape them for this and other purposes). Most textbooks in informal logic have a section on loaded language, and exercises to practice identifying and avoiding it. While you're at it, warn students against some of the other classical fallacies in informal logic (lists may be found in any informal logic book—for example my *Rulebook for Arguments* [Indianapolis: Hackett, 1987, 1992] or Howard Kahane's *Logic and Contemporary Rhetoric* [Belmont, Ca: Wadsworth, many editions]). These fallacies are all too easy to illustrate using popular writings on any of the current ethical issues. The habit of analyzing ethical arguments on their merits and stating them fairly, even if we don't agree with them, comes as a shock to many students, but for precisely that reason it is crucial.

The other great danger is rationalization. When we rationalize, we persuade ourselves that we *are* thinking about ethics—offering and weighing various reasons—even when we are mainly just making excuses and trying to save face. It may be hard to see. As Freud once said, when it comes to self-justification, we're all geniuses.

Still, there are some strategies to try. Help students learn to watch themselves—to watch, for example, for that telltale anger or irritation at being challenged. Point out that we often find ourselves becoming irritated or angry when our especially precious excuses are too persistently or effectively challenged by someone else. The clever part, the evasion, is that we get angry at the person challenging us, rather than considering that we might really be at fault for offering an offhand excuse in the first place.

So watch for the automatic counterattack. Go back to the class debate videos (here I find it useful to use videos of other classes so that students aren't put on the spot). Ask whether, when a person is listening to someone else, he or she is trying to understand or just waiting for the speaker to stop so that he or she can give a comeback. Are they trying to win, or to learn? Practice responding in more constructive and careful ways: summarizing the other side's points to their satisfaction, for example, before responding (and then expecting the same consideration in return). Nothing is so effective at disrupting the habits of offhandedness that make rationalizing and dogmatism possible. An engaging and readily teachable book on this subject is Tom Rusk, *The Power of Ethical Persuasion* (New York: Penguin, 1993).

A new generation of critical thinking texts by philosophers addresses the psychological issues raised here: the attitudes and practices that stand in the way of clear and careful thinking. Most notably see Vincent Ruggerio, *Beyond Feelings: A Guide to Critical Thinking* (Mountain View, CA: Mayfield, 1995)—a critical thinking text that actually begins with the question "Who Are You?".

Chapter 2: Appeal to authority is usually discussed as a fallacy in informal logic texts. It is also sometimes not a fallacy, as I point out in my *Rulebook for Arguments*. You might point out that it seldom works in ethics, though, both because putative ethical authorities disagree and, more fundamentally, because the grounds of their allegedly special ethical expertise are seldom clear, which is not always the case with nonethical claims.

You might propose a bit of historical research. Look into what the (so-called) experts have said about the future (how often were they right?), or what doctors have said over the decades about how to be healthy, or how often political leaders claim that "God is on our side" when pounding the drums of war. It's amusing when our bumper stickers say that God is on the side of our favorite college football team. It's not so amusing when we claim, in the same spirit, that God is on the side of our country in some international face-off. God should be spoken for with a little more modesty. Some exposure to the history of such appeals may help us identify and challenge them when they confront us in our own lives.

End this discussion constructively. Point out to students that although appeals to authority are generally not acceptable in ethics, this does not somehow leave us with nothing to say. We are instead invited to offer our own reasons for our ethical views, and usually this is not hard to do. Go back even to the putative authorities: they usually offer reasons too. Students can adopt and adapt them. Stress the adaptation part. We may adopt others' arguments, but it is still our responsibility to make those arguments our own: adding evidence, for example, considering counterevidence, and continuing to be open to other points of view. It may be entirely possible to argue, for instance, that our country's position in some international face-off is justified. The point is that it takes some argument to show this.

Chapter 3: Creative problem-solving methods can be productively practiced in class. All of De Bono's methods, for example, can be modeled in class: the intermediate impossible, brainstorming, random word association. For random word association, I have my class select some ethical issue, divide into groups, pick some word at random out of whatever printed material is at hand, and then explore any new perspectives on the problem, or possible new solutions to it, that the randomly selected words suggest.

In the face of the Heinz dilemma, for example, you might turn to the dictionary for random associations. When I did it, the first word I found was "oboe." "Oboe?", I said to myself. "You've got to be kidding!" Then I thought: Well, an oboe is a musical instrument; an oboe-like instrument is used to charm cobras in India; maybe Heinz could somehow charm the druggist? How? Well, I'm not sure, but it seems worthwhile for Heinz at least to talk to the druggist again.

Back to oboes. People play such instruments; people have skills; Heinz has skills: aha! This is how I first reached the idea of bartering skills for the drug. The next word I found was "leaf." "Turn over a new leaf"? "Read leaves"? (Foretelling the future, as people used to do with tea leaves? Let's see: how do we know that this drug is any good . . . ?) Use leaves instead of drugs? (Are there herbal remedies . . . ?).

In this way, the class can see that even such improbable methods actually work—in fact, work well. I usually follow up with a short quiz in which students are given another ethical problem and asked again to generate new ideas and approaches to it.

Practice some of the other techniques as well. I should add that what I say in the text only scratches the surface of the problem-solving literature. Don't overlook the references in the Notes and Comments for Chapter 3. An entire course could be devoted just to this theme.

Chapter 4: To open the question of polarized values, have students do bumper sticker surveys. They are a striking way to illustrate how thoroughly polarized our thinking sometimes gets. Also, new ideas and approaches sometimes come up. If you live in a politically homogeneous area, you might want to supplement the usual bumper stickers with your own selections from catalogs.

Integrative approaches need modeling and practice. For example, select an ethical issue and divide the class into groups. First ask the students to list all of the ethical values they think are at stake in the situation. Then ask them to work out an approach to the issue—a compromise, a middle way, or a more creatively integrative solution—that aims to harmonize the different values at stake rather than insisting that only a few are right. Another possibility is to ask students to write and perform short dialogues illustrating polarized and integrative approaches to certain issues. The polarized dialogues are usually enjoyable (no weapon is as effective as laughter), though they can occasionally be raw as well. Either way, the class then turns to the integrative approach with relief and seriousness.

Polarized thinking closes questions. An integrative approach, by contrast, needn't arrive at a definite answer. Its attitude—open-ended, exploratory, willing to listen rather than sloganize—is what is crucial. This too may come as a surprise to students. You might note this surprise and even make a point of it. Integrative thinking is not at all as widely practiced as it ought to be.

I have tried ending this section of the course by returning to the bumper sticker project with a new assignment: design integrative bumper stickers (such as "Every child a wanted child"). At the very least this leads to interesting discussions!

Chapter 5: There are effective ways to illustrate and expose stereotyping and other means of closing the heart. For example, the objectification of women in advertisements is the subject of a powerful short film by Jean Kilbourne, *Still Killing Us Softly* (available from Cambridge Documentary Films, P.O. Box 385, Cambridge, MA 02139). After watching the film, students can be asked to find and analyze their own examples: they're as close as the nearest newsstand. Then broaden the discussion to other forms of objectification.

The self-fulfilling effects of stereotyping might be driven home by assigning students stereotyped roles (perhaps after together listing some features of the usual stereotypes on the board) and role-playing some interaction, such as a business meeting, job interview, or news show. Put the stereotype label on a headband or sticker so that the person being stereotyped doesn't know what label he or she wears—then observe how this person's behavior is changed anyway. Ask how the person feels. Videotape these sessions if possible; then the class can analyze the tape. You might also want to discuss the effects of stereotyping and other forms of heart closing right at home: in the classroom, for example.

When my introductory course includes Singer's *Animal Liberation*, I ask the students, as an opening exercise, to imagine themselves in a situation where space aliens propose to do to us what we do to other animals. The students then have to try to find some reasons that might persuade the aliens (role-played by other students from the class) not to factory-farm humans for food, while explaining why it is ethically acceptable for humans to factory-farm animals (or else proposing a change in this human behavior). Other students role-play animals—to keep the humans honest. Sometimes we have open-court hearings, in costume. It's fun—but the underlying point, and challenge, are powerful and memorable. We rarely put ourselves in the place of other animals.

We can practice open-hearted attentiveness too, right in the classroom. Indeed, we must, if we are to mean what we say. For one example of how, see Tangren Alexander, "The

Womanly Art of Teaching Ethics, or One Fruitful Way to Encourge the Love of Wisdom about Right and Wrong," in *Teaching Philosophy* 10:4 (1987), pp. 319-328. Alexander writes of her class:

> Being heard; that's a lot of what this class is about. Learning to get and to give a respectful hearing. Learning to speak out about what we know of right and wrong, learning to say our say, and to listen to others. I do what I can to build trust among us. I encourage risk-taking by taking risks myself. I try to create an atmosphere of safety for speaking out. (p. 322)

Simple stuff—but hard to build into a course, and too rarely tried.

My colleague John Sullivan asks his students to *bow* to each other in small groups—silently, slowly, maintaining eye contact, one by one. It is an exercise that they find nearly impossible the first time. But they do understand it, and eventually they learn to live up to their understanding of it. Part of what they begin to recognize is how habitually we usually relate to each other, barely pausing to hear, let alone appreciate, anyone else. It is another exercise that seems to stay with people long after the theories and the arguments have faded from mind.

You might consider a joint class service project as well, undertaken during the term and reflected upon together at the end. Ram Dass and Paul Gorman's book *How Can I Help?* (New York: Knopf, 1985) is an inspiring and philosophically compelling discussion of service work.

These are, of course, just a few examples of what might be done with this material. Different instructors will use this book very differently. Let me just add that I would be most grateful to hear about any exercises or applications of this material that worked well for you—or any other suggestions about how this book could be more helpful. I wish you the best of luck.